What Others Are Saying About Larry and Tiz Huch
and *Releasing Family Blessings...*

Though civilization depends upon it, raising a family in accordance with God's biblical blueprint is becoming ever more challenging. The love, the stability, the harmony, and the tranquility of the Torah-true home cocoons parents and children alike in a nurturing, secure environment. My friends Larry and Tiz Huch provide much-needed advice in their new book for all those struggling against the odds to build beautiful families.

—*Rabbi Daniel Lapin*
American Alliance of Jews and Christians

Pastors Tiz and Larry are great examples of God's awesome love and mercy. Their book will be a lifesaver to hurting marriages and will bless multitudes. I salute them for writing it.

—*Dodie Osteen*
Cofounder of Lakewood Church
Houston, Texas

We have known Larry and Tiz Huch for many years and consider them very dear friends. They are a powerful couple in the kingdom—highly effective pastors, Bible teachers, television hosts, and authors who are loved and respected by many around the world. They have built a strong marriage and family with children who not only embrace the ministry but work alongside them in it. We applaud them on their collaborative effort in *Releasing Family Blessings*. This book reveals biblical secrets that create a bridge of instruction and encouragement for others to walk over and into God's plan for the family.

—*Marcus and Joni Lamb*
Founders, Daystar Television Network

We encourage you to read this exciting book drawn from the waters of the authors' own experience in their successful marriage and close-knit family. We know that Larry and Tiz are dedicated partners in a marriage, a fact that places an umbrella of security around their family, a shield of protection under God's wing, and a purposeful vision for all. *Releasing Family Blessings* is a must-read!

—*Martin and Shaneen Clarke*
International Director, Full Gospel Business Men's Fellowship International;
Founder, Shaneen Clarke Ministries
London, United Kingdom

I've had one pastor for over twenty years: Larry Huch. He is a phenomenal leader, teacher, and friend. His revelations and spiritual insight into the Jewish roots of Christianity and breaking family curses have changed my life and family. One of the main reasons we have personally stayed connected to pastors Larry and Tiz is because of their leadership in the area of marriage and family. They have always pressed into God for His way of living life, and their family is the proof and their reward. *Releasing Family Blessings* walks us through the points they have learned along the way and, like all of their books, is destined to be an instant classic.

—*Scott Sigman*
Director, Larry Huch Ministries
Associate Pastor, DFW New Beginnings
Irving, Texas

Releasing
FAMILY BLESSINGS

Releasing FAMILY BLESSINGS

LARRY & TIZ HUCH

WHITAKER
HOUSE

RELEASING FAMILY BLESSINGS:
God's Plan for Your Marriage and Children

Larry and Tiz Huch
P.O. Box 610890
Dallas, TX 75261
www.newbeginnings.org / www.LarryHuchMinistries.com / www.TizHuch.com

ISBN: 978-1-60374-554-3
Printed in the United States of America
© 2012 by Larry and Tiz Huch

Whitaker House
1030 Hunt Valley Circle
New Kensington, PA 15068
www.whitakerhouse.com

Library of Congress Cataloging-in-Publication Data

Huch, Larry.
  Releasing family blessings / by Larry and Tiz Huch.
    p. cm.
  Summary: "The authors share biblical wisdom and practical tips gleaned from thirty-five-plus years of marriage and ministry together to demonstrate how to build a strong, healthy, happy family by doing it God's way"—Provided by publisher.
  ISBN 978-1-60374-554-3 (trade pbk. : alk. paper) 1. Marriage—Religious aspects—Christianity. 2. Families—Religious aspects—Christianity. 3. Home—Religious aspects—Christianity. I. Huch, Tiz, 1956– II. Title.
  BV835.H75 2012
  248.4—dc23
                                    2012021972

2 3 4 5 6 7 8 9 10 11   W   18 17 16 15 14 13 12

Dedication

This book is dedicated to our kids and our grandkids, the "Sugars," who are the light of our lives. You are the living demonstration of the blessings of God in our family. Every day, you fill our lives with joy, love, and meaning. We are so proud of each one of you, and we have loved watching your individual gifts develop into the destiny the Lord has for you. As you honor the Lord, He honors you. You amaze us continually!

We also want to dedicate this book to the "people for our lives"—our staff, our friends, and the thousands of people who allow us to be their pastors, their spiritual parents, and their guild.

To all of our family and friends, "Our best is yet to come!"

Contents

Foreword

FROM THE KIDS

As a wife and a mother of three, I understand the challenges of balancing all the daily issues of life. I find myself always coming back to the question, What are my true priorities? I look back and see the incredible effort my parents always made to teach my brother, my sister, and me about what was really important: God, family, people, and character. It wasn't enough to simply take us to church. They taught us the meaning of those values through constant conversation. They led us by example, and we followed. We learned at their knees the true meaning of compassion for others, service, character, and passion for the kingdom of God. Those fundamental values keep our family working, loving, and living in harmony today.

The book you're about to read doesn't just contain tips for families but the true values that built a solid foundation for us—the values that keep a family together for life. My hope is that in this book, you'll find tools for building a strong, happy, God-centered family, just as I am doing as I implement these teachings in my own family.

—*Anna Huch-Reed*
(Eldest daughter of Larry and Tiz)

Life gives us the chance to pursue so many things: fame, fortune, success, social status. We have so many opportunities, but to me, there is nothing as important as family. Nothing compares with the joy and love I am rewarded with because of my family. Family is something to belong to; something bigger than yourself—your family is there to help you when you're down, to share laughter with, and to build a life with. This is why I love my family so much—why I spend so much time with them and am always surrounded by them. There is no such thing as a perfect family, but there are steps we can take and lessons we can learn to strengthen our families and improve our relationships. By taking the time to read this book, you are making an investment in your family's future. To me, there is no greater investment than that! God bless.

—Brandin Reed
(Husband of Anna/son-in-law of Larry and Tiz)

The strongest influence a child will even encounter is the influence of his parents, because a parent's interpretation of the world becomes the foundation of that child's character. Therefore, concerning family, proper influence is the greatest responsibility and opportunity a parent will ever have. As a child gets older, character development becomes more and more his own responsibility, and eventually, every child will choose whether to water the roots established by his family unit or to let them wither and die.

This book presents the very heart of my parents and their biblical view of family. It will help parents learn how to have a powerful influence on their children's lives at every stage and to impart godly character, which is the foundation of every great family. I thank my mother and father for never allowing circumstances to determine their character and for influencing my character through their example. I also congratulate them on this book. I know it will be a blessing to all who read it and put its wisdom into practice.

—Luke Huch
(Middle son of Larry and Tiz)

God truly handpicked my in-laws, pastors Larry and Tiz Huch, to be the light to all of our families by releasing this powerful book full of insightful words of wisdom on the family. I'm so blessed to have the opportunity to have them as my parents. I have experienced firsthand what it's like to marry into a family full of joy and blessings and to have the most motivating, inspiring, wonderful, generous, kind, loving in-laws, who always take the time to spend quality family time together with all of us. They are genuinely committed to having a family that serves as an example of God's love to the world. I am forever thankful for the impact they have made, and continue to make, on my life. I have been given one of the best parts of them: my wonderful husband, Luke—their son—who brings me great joy and love, just like his parents. I love you guys forever!

—Jennifer Huch
(Wife of Luke/daughter-in-law of Larry and Tiz)

When you're little, you think every other family is just like yours. Then, as you grow, you see that your mom and dad are something special. When I was in high school, particularly when we moved to Texas, it finally clicked for me. My parents raised us in a unique way—they lived every day what they preached. They held high standards, they set guidelines, and there were no exceptions. Even in my "free-spirited" teenage years, if I didn't agree with a certain rule, I knew deep down that they were right and had my best interests at heart.

I knew from a young age that I was blessed to have parents who loved me enough to tell me no sometimes. They taught us that God has a plan and a pathway for the family, and I watched them walk daily and direct us with the guidelines of how our family was to function. We knew that, as children of God, we were set apart and had a big calling on our lives. I saw my parents support each other not only in church, spiritually, but also in our family and in business. My dad was my mom's biggest fan; she was his greatest cheerleader. He showed us how a man should treat his wife—loving, supporting, and encouraging her. She showed us how a wife should treat her husband—respecting him, honoring him, and having his back, no matter what. They taught us by *showing* us.

They've always supported each other and all of us kids. We always knew we were loved, we knew we were covered, and we knew we had responsibilities to them and to God. They always imparted the vision that we were to lead by example—that we are leaders, not followers! They taught us to dream big, to work hard, and to play even harder. They taught us that God comes first, then family, then friends, then ministry. They showed us guidelines to walk by daily and throughout life. They gave me a truth-based blueprint of how to live as a young Christian woman, and they also gave me a great vision for my future family. What a blessing and an honor to have them as parents and to be working with them in the ministry today!

Releasing Family Blessings really shows how our family works. It offers an inside view of how my parents think, how they speak, how they pray, and, most important, how they live. I know you will love this book! It is real and practical—a great guide to having a great family.

—*Katie Huch*
(Youngest daughter of Larry and Tiz/"the baby of the family")

Preface

We have wanted to write a book on the family for a long time. For the past thirty-five years, we have been privileged to participate in the adventures that are marriage and full-time ministry. We have pioneered seven different churches, two of which were in Australia, within a six-year period; we have ministered in many nations across the globe, to nearly every nationality and race; we film a television program, *New Beginnings*, and have published several books, all which reach practically every corner of the world. We have had the honor of leading thousands of people to the Lord. We have the greatest job in the world—connecting people to God, to His Word and its promises, and to His miracle power!

We have spent our lives striving to make an impact on the world as the Lord leads us. But our accomplishments in ministry can never compare to the joy we find in our family, which we will always consider to be our greatest achievement by far. And it's where we've had the greatest impact for the Lord.

We are blessed to be the parents of three grown children, who, along with their spouses, love the Lord with all their hearts and are active in ministry with us. We have three grandchildren, the "Sugars," who are the light of our lives. We truly enjoy one another. Perhaps one of the reasons we treasure our family so much is because we weren't always this way. Believe us when we say that the road to marital bliss was marked by much toil and many learning experiences. But it's these experiences that qualify us to share with you now some keys to success in your own family.

Several years ago, we met a young couple who were in the ministry—and, sadly, on the verge of divorce. They were facing seemingly irreconcilable differences and had given up hope that their marriage could ever change for the better. Our hearts went out to them, and we decided to fly them in to spend a few days with us. During our time together, we listened to them, counseled them, broke the curses off of their lives, and prayed with them for God's healing and restoration in their marriage and ministry.

Long story short, the Lord worked a miracle and turned their marriage around! Today, they have a happy marriage, a wonderful family, and a thriving church. And we were blessed to have had a hand in this blessed outcome.

Back when we were counseling them, through her tears, the wife asked me, "Why have you spent all of this money, time, and effort on us? Why do you even care about us?" I answered her simply, "Because we've been there, ourselves."

Today, we say the same thing to you: we've been where you are. We have faced what you are facing, or something similar. We have felt the hopelessness. We have been on the verge of giving up on our marriage. We have agonized over hurts, sorrows, and pains. We have faced obstacles and challenges that seemed insurmountable. We have cried tears of loneliness and wondered if anybody cared. We have experienced emotional damage from which we thought we'd never recover. We have been on the verge of giving up on our marriage. We have faced obstacles and challenges that seemed insurmountable. We know, from personal experience and from years of pastoring, the downward spiral that negative emotions can take.

That's why we wrote this book—to testify how far God has brought us, so that you'll find assurance that He's taking you great places, too!

We also know where you've been in the adventure of parenting. Our kids are grown now, but while we were raising them, we often wondered if we were making the right decisions. Most parents probably second-guess a lot of their parenting choices. Are we being too strict? Are we being too liberal? Should we push them harder or lighten up? Are we expecting too much or too little?

Successful parenting requires many things, including commitment, patience, and—most important—lots of prayer! In the coming chapters, we will guild you and pray you through much of these issues.

In the ancient Hebrew language, there is no word for "coincidence." We believe it's no coincidence you're reading this book right now! We didn't write this book just to inform you but rather to *transform* you. In it, we will teach you foundational principles from God's Word, as well as practical wisdom from thirty-five-plus years of experience in marriage, family management, and ministry. We will show you how to bring timeless truths from ancient biblical wisdom into the reality of your everyday lives in order to release the blessings God has promised for your marriage, your children, and your home!

We have written *Releasing Family Blessings* in a "he said, she said" format, in an effort to share our own perspectives on the principles and practices we present. One of the biggest challenges we faced in writing this book was to decide what to include. Marriage and family are such broad topics, and it's impossible to cover everything we have to say in one book. So, we tried to squeeze in as much as possible, with the promise that we'd write a sequel, if necessary, for anything we might have forgotten.

Our goal is to impart timeless biblical wisdom to you and enable you to apply it in a practical way to your situation in order to strengthen your marriage, build up your family, and fill your home with the peace, joy, and love of God.

We will also teach you how to…

- safeguard your marriage
- protect your children from the enemy's attack
- get "past" your past
- rebound from mistakes
- resolve conflicts and overcome differences
- set healthy boundaries for your children
- enforce godly discipline
- bring God's presence, light, and joy into your heart and home

At the end of each chapter, we will give you an easy-to-follow synopsis and application plan. Then, we will lead you in a powerful prayer to break off the chains and burdens of the past and set you free into God's wonderful future for you and your family. Join us as we begin this journey together!

—Pastors Larry and Tiz Huch

Introduction

CHANGING THE WORLD STARTS AT HOME

Perhaps the greatest social service that can be rendered by anybody to
this country and to mankind is to bring up a family.
—George Bernard Shaw

She said:

Everything that exists started out as a plan from the mind of the Master Architect, God Himself. When He spoke the world into existence, He did so based on a precise blueprint designed to keep everything in perfect alignment. And everything that God created was "good"—perfect, complete. How do we know? Because He called His creation "good" seven times! (See Genesis 1:4, 10, 12, 18, 21, 25, 31.) In fact, He called it *"very good"* in Genesis 1:31.

Every component of His creation completely fulfilled the purposes for which He designed it. Each part reflected His glory and portrayed his nature, majesty, and power. The psalmist wrote, *"The heavens declare the glory of God; the skies proclaim the work of his hands"* (Psalm 19:1 NIV).

The second chapter of Genesis gives us a detailed description of the process by which God created mankind, and the only thing that was *"not good"* (Genesis 2:18) was the fact that man was alone. So, God gave to Adam a helper—a soul mate, a life companion, a lover—in the person of Eve, and He made provision for them to procreate: *"God blessed them and said to them, 'Be fruitful and increase in number; fill the earth and subdue it'"* (Genesis 1:28 NIV). This was the crowning moment of creation: the formation of the first family!

From the very beginning, God ordained that the family unit of husband, wife, and children should be the most important institution on earth—the vessel through which God would extend His dominion over the earth. Godly families were then, and are still today, God's chosen way to change the world.

The State of the Family

What is the state of this all-important institution today? Sadly, the family—God's chosen vessel of world transformation—has been gravely cheapened. Recently, a woman told me that her son had gotten a girl pregnant, and she said, "Thank goodness he's finally pulling himself together for the sake of the baby." This is becoming more and more commonplace—unmarried couples casually having babies without a solid foundation in their lives. Children are a sacred gift entrusted to their parents by the Lord, and it's heartbreaking to think about the nonchalance with which many young people approach pregnancy and parenting nowadays.

Much of this decline is due to the influence of the media. Twenty years ago, you never would have seen a TV episode or a movie scene depicting a man, a woman, and a bed together in the same room at the same time. Today, anything goes. Now, I'm not out to condemn anyone or to rant and rave, only to point out that the family has fallen from its place of sanctity in the minds of many people.

The Effects of "Expert" Advice

It's time for new role models to emerge— godly husbands and wives who commit to their marriages and collaborate to raise their kids.

Celebrities, media moguls, and relationship "experts" have plenty of advice on how to manage our families. I was scanning the TV channels recently and stumbled upon a talk show on which the four female hosts were talking about marriage. One of them declared that monogamous marriage was an old-fashioned, outdated notion that was irrelevant in today's society. She went on to say that if she were ever to get married, she would tell her husband upfront that she could not guarantee she'd be faithful to him alone. These experts would have us say "I do" and then keep the back door open to other relationships. Meanwhile, many of them have gotten divorced and remarried so many times, they've lost track.

Tragically, with "role models" such as these, countless men and women end up in all kinds of relationships that leave pieces of their hearts scattered all over the place, and they can't recognize Mr. Right when he finally comes along. There is too much at stake to follow the advice of somebody who's headed down the path of failure. The real tragedy is that they are leading multitudes down the same path. It's time for new role models to emerge—not Hollywood couples who continually divorce and remarry, but godly husbands and wives who commit to their marriages and collaborate to raise their kids.

He said:

It's true that the family receives all sorts of messages, advice, and examples that are not from God. The world has all manner of "wisdom" on how our homes ought to be. Secular society preaches at us through sitcoms, movies, magazines, and the like. However, the methods man approves often lead to destruction, as the book of Proverbs attests: *"There is a way that seems right to a man, but its end is the way of death"* (Proverbs 14:12; 16:25).

In Ephesians 6:11, the apostle Paul exhorts us to *"stand against the wiles ["schemes" NIV] of the devil."* The devil is subtle and cunning in his schemes to destroy the family. Of course, if you were watching a show on television, and the host suddenly sprouted horns and was wielding a pitchfork, you would probably say, "I'm not going to listen to her." But the devil isn't going to say, "Listen to me, and I'll tell you how to ruin your life." No one would fall for his schemes! Instead, he works subtly, through movies, television shows, and other media; he speaks through certain rock stars, pop artists, politicians, and other celebrity figures.

> *We need to be wary of basing our lives, our marriages, and our families on what our culture says.*

Now, I'm not saying that a specific person is the devil, only that the devil uses people—even people who have good intentions. We need to be wary of basing our lives, our marriages, and our families on what our culture says. Moreover, the opinions of the so-called experts will change, while God's Word never changes.

God's Word: Our Ultimate Authority

On vacation, I played a few rounds of golf with my son-in-law. If I may say so, I played really well—better than I'd played in years. For a while, I'd gotten so frustrated with my game that I'd considered giving it up for good. But then I saw something on the Golf Channel that made me realize I had been gripping the club all wrong. Three years prior, a golf expert had told me to change my grip. I had done as he suggested—and wasn't able to play after that.

Life often works the same way. Somebody says, "This is the way you ought to live life," "This is how you should raise your family," "This is the secret to a happy

> *God is the final authority when it comes to interacting with our spouses and raising our children.*

marriage," and so forth. But if the advice doesn't correspond to the wisdom we get from the Expert, our heavenly Father, then it won't work. He wrote the Book, and we need to live according to His rules if we want to be blessed.

As the Creator of everything, including marriage and families, God is the final authority when it comes to interacting with our spouses and raising our children. We may be in the world, but we are not of the world. (See John 15:19; 17:14; James 4:4.) Therefore, the world is not our authority on how to run our homes. The Word of God alone offers the timeless truths that will guide us to success in getting along with our spouses, raising our children, and managing our households.

She said:

We can change the world around us, as God equips us. He does not expect us to solve every world crisis, but He does expect us to resolve the crises in our homes. Praise God, we aren't on our own—He has left us a plan for the family, a blueprint to follow. And it's called the Bible—the Word of God. It's in this Manual of time-tested truths for building a life that's marked by integrity, making a marriage that lasts, and raising godly children who will not depart from our teachings that we learn about the path God has established for us. He does not want our families and marriages to fall apart. He wants us to be set apart—different from the rest of the world. Other people should look at us and say, "There's something different about you and your kids."

It's for our own good that God gives us a path to walk upon. He didn't establish a bunch of rules and regulations to keep us restricted. His laws are meant to protect us and give us lives that are healthy, productive, and blessed—not self-destructive. The enemy is a thief and a robber who seeks to destroy us, but Jesus came to give us *"life…more abundantly"* (John 10:10). God wants to breathe His breath of everlasting life into our marriages, our families, and our children. And He never points a finger of condemnation; He only reaches out a hand to pull us off of our self-destructive detours and to set us on the path to our divine destinies.

Trust in the God of Mercy

If we mess up, we simply start over again, because God is a God of restoration. Some of the greatest marriages I know were reassembled by God after a painful divorce. His grace is unending, His mercies never failing. Other people may say, "You'll never make it. You'll never amount to anything. You'll always be this way. Your parents were that way. Your mom was that way, and your dad was that way; you're going to be the same way." But the Lord takes that old script, wads it up in a ball, and throws it out. Then, He writes a brand-new script for our lives.

It's up to us to grab ahold of that script—to step into it and make it ours. It's almost overwhelming to think of all of the opportunities God brings our way, if we'll only be ready for them. Too often, we simply sit back and remain in "coasting" mode. Some people wait their whole lives for their ship to come in, while other people swim out to meet it. The Word of God contains thousands of promises guaranteeing us great families and miraculous blessings, but it isn't like the lottery; we can't just sit back and wait for Ed McMahon to show up at the door. We need to go after the promises and seize them! We do that by taking the Word of God and proclaiming it over our lives every day.

Heal the World, One Home at a Time

It's an age-old question: What can we do to make America a better country? This query was posed countless times to former First Lady Barbara Bush as she traveled around the nation for speaking engagements. Do you know how she responded? "My greatest role in creating the future of the United States is to tell parents to raise good children. If we raise great kids, we will have a great nation." Her conviction was echoed by Pope John Paul II, who said, "As the family goes, so goes the nation, and so goes the whole world in which we live."

"As the family goes, so goes the nation, and so goes the whole world in which we live."

Whatever happens in the home is exported out into the world—reproduced, whether for good or for bad. This is why the way we treat our spouses, raise our children, and manage our households is so important. While there are a lot of areas over which we have no control, we do have control over how we treat our spouses, what we teach our children, and the degree to which our family represents the light of God to the world. If we will work toward strengthening our marriages, our children, and our families, we will strengthen the fiber of society and promote the strengthening of other marriages and families. It's true: changing the world has to start at home.

We have this charge in Deuteronomy 6:6–9:

And these words which I command you today shall be in your heart. You shall teach them diligently to your children, and shall talk of them when you sit in your house, when you walk by the way, when you lie down, and when you rise up. You shall bind them as a sign on your hand, and they shall be as frontlets between your eyes. You shall write them on the doorposts of your house and on your gates.

God is not interested in merely blessing us—He's interested in setting a pattern for the rest of the world. The promises He made to Abraham weren't just for him but also for the generations to come. And God wants to set this pattern through our families.

He said:

Tiz and I love to study the Jewish roots of the Christian faith. There is such a wealth of knowledge and wisdom that has changed our lives and family drastically for the better! One of the greatest truths we have discovered is that God has a purpose for us in this life. Each of us has a God-given mission to make the world a better place—to practice *tikkun olam*, the Hebrew term for healing and repairing the world.

This may sound like a daunting mission, but it's simple, really, when we remember that it starts with our families. We can change the world, one family at a time! And that's precisely the way God intends us to go about it. When we keep His commandments and also teach them to our children, His ways and will get passed down from generation to generation, as they simultaneously spread to our own neighborhoods, communities, cities, states, and nations. The Word of God, and its power to bring hope and healing, will be reproduced in our own lives, as well as in the lives of our descendants for generations and generations. This is the key to releasing God's blessings into your family and throughout the world!

Transformed, Step-by-Step

She said:

As you are on this journey, keep this in mind: we are going to take you one step at a time. It has been said that there is no elevator to success. There is only a stairway that takes you step-by-step. That's absolutely true, and it's crucial to keep in mind, or you'll risk becoming overwhelmed.

I don't know your situation right now. Maybe your marriage is sailing on smooth waters, or maybe you're being tossed by the waves of conflict and upheaval. Maybe you would go so far as to say your family is shipwrecked—or sunk. Let me encourage you today—God has great plans for you and your future! He cares deeply about the family, in general, and your family, in particular. In fact, your family is on His mind right now! (See Psalm 115:12.) His desire is to bless you, your children, and your children's children, for generations to come, and to guide them along His path to peace, prosperity, and joy. This path is laid out in His Word, the Holy Bible—a real Book with real answers for real life.

The Bible has been our primary resource as we've endeavored to follow the Lord's plan for the family. The important thing to remember is that the Bible isn't a bunch of do's and don'ts; it's a path designed to position you to receive God's best. And it isn't based on performance but on grace. Transforming our families is a step-by-step process!

Let me share a story to encourage you in this regard. Years ago, a man named Joe was invited to our church. Joe had grown up in a dysfunctional family. His father had abused him physically, and he had no concept of parental love—a father's love, in particular. During a service at our church, Joe surrendered his life to the Lord. His salvation was dramatic in that he was set free from a drug addiction, but he still struggled with a sense of self-condemnation and found it hard to accept that God loved him. He was dynamically saved and set free from drugs and addictions, but he struggled with self condemnation and acceptance that the Lord loved him.

One day at church, he had a breakthrough in this area. Before I found out what had happened, I noticed a physical difference—he was smiling and full of joy. He later told me that he'd had a tough week at work and had lost his temper with several coworkers. He had been miserable, suffering from the heavy weight of condemnation, as well as from a hopeless sense that the Lord was angry with him—and always would be, because he could never really change. He hadn't felt like coming to church that day, but he came, anyway.

As he was holding hands with his two-year-old son to walk him up the balcony stairs, the little boy stumbled. Joe told me he instinctively lifted his son to the step, as any father would do, and kept walking. In that moment, the Lord spoke to his heart and said, "That's exactly how I react to you, My son. As you are trying to climb to the next step of your life, if you stumble, I am holding your hand and will lift you up to the next step. Then, together, we just keep on walking and moving forward and upward." Joe realized that the love he had for his son mirrored the love God had for him and all of His children. And that realization changed his life!

Let the Lord touch your heart right now with that same love. No matter who you are, where you came from, or where you find yourself today, your heavenly Father loves you and has a wonderful destiny in store for you! As He takes you step-by-step toward that destiny, celebrate every victory along the way, no matter how small. If you make a mistake, do your best to fix it, get back up, and start again. If you make another mistake, repeat the process!

Success is not a destination; it's a journey. As you read this book, open your heart to the Lord. Let Him flood your soul with hope, understanding, direction, and faith. Let Him begin to bring fresh insight, help, and favor into your marriage and family. Make a new commitment to God, yourself and your family that you are going to become the absolute best version of yourself! Let the Lord breathe His breath of life into your heart, soul, and mind. Let His Spirit fill your home with His presence, His joy, and His light! Get ready to take a breath of fresh air—it's time for a new beginning!

Prayer

Let's pray together to kick off our journey and release the blessings of God on your family.

Father God, we come to You in the name and the power of Jesus Christ, our Lord and Savior. We open our hearts to You, Lord. Flood our souls with hope, understanding, direction, and faith. Bring us fresh insights. Shower Your favor on our marriages and families.

Today, Lord, we commit to becoming the best version of ourselves, through Your divine help and equipping. We surrender our hearts, our lives, and our families to You, and we ask You to breathe Your breath of life into us. Create in us a clean heart and renew Your Spirit within us. Make our homes into sanctuaries filled with Your love, hope, faith, joy, and peace. And help each of us to be a light in our homes. Use us to bring healing to a hurting world, starting with our own families. Raise up a heart of courage, strength, and faith within us to stand against the attacks of the enemy.

Right now, we break every generational curse on our lives, our families, and our homes. At the same time, we release every blessing, every stored up blessing from God into us, for us, and through us! Bless us greatly, Lord, so that we may be a great blessing to the world and especially to our own families! In Jesus' name, amen.

PART I:

Release Blessings on Your Marriage

Chapter 1

What the Lord Has Done for Us, He Will Do for You!

What greater thing is there for two human souls than to feel that they are joined for life—to strengthen each other in all labor, to rest on each other in all sorrow, to minister to each other in all pain, to be one with each other in silent, unspeakable memories?
—George Eliot

He said:

Tiz and I just celebrated our thirty-fifth wedding anniversary, praise God, and in our years of marriage and ministry together, we have learned a thing or two. Our relationship started out on a rough and rocky road, but, by the grace of God, as well as through our own personal growth, we learned how to build a strong marriage and a solid family. Today, we are happier than we have ever could have hoped to be, we're enjoying life more than ever before, and our ministry is more fruitful than it has ever been. We also know that our best days are still ahead of us!

We share these things not to flaunt or brag, but to encourage you—what the Lord has done for us and our family, He will do for you, too! And we're committed to helping that happen. For years, we have counseled couples and taught on breaking generational curses and releasing family blessings. We have seen hundreds of thousands of lives changed, marriages saved, and families helped and made whole by the power of God. That's why we're excited about this book—it's a way to show countless more couples and families how to break the curse and unleash the blessing! Our intent is not to fill your head with teachings but to fill your heart with hope and faith that you, too, can transform your life, your marriage, and your family. Our hope is that you will view our experiences as a bridge over the rocky places of past mistakes and onto the smoothly paved Promised Land of God's covenant blessings.

Worldly Advice Versus Biblical Wisdom

She said:

I know that most people want to be happy; to have the best marriages possible; and to raise happy, healthy children who rise up and call them blessed. Those who aren't married yet probably hope to have a happy marriage someday. And these are some of the wonderful things God has in store for us! Yet we live in a world that gives us all kinds of alternative options. Some people say, "I have the right to do this or that," or "I'm living in liberty. I'm just going to do what feels good." The Bible says that there is a way that seems right to man, but it ends in destruction. (See Proverbs 14:12.) Unfortunately, secular values and worldly "morals" have bled over into the Christian faith, to a large degree. We rarely hear about anyone desiring to stay on the path, even in church. I don't know about you, but if someone can save me from a lot of heartache, I want to hear what he has to say. I want to learn from those who have done it right and found success.

Now, Larry and I won't claim to be experts in the realms of marriage and family. We have a great marriage and a wonderful family, true, but only because of the One who designed marriage in the first place. Our relationship is truly a living testament to the power of God. Sometimes, I just have to sit down and take a deep breath when I think about where God has brought Larry and me. We've proven that He can take two independent, stubborn, angry, messy people, bring them together in marriage, and create a beautiful relationship out of it. God has taken the traumas we've been through and turned them into a sense of compassion for others—a desire to see them through the same problems.

Even though Larry and I became Christians around the same time, our testimonies were completely unique, and our backgrounds could not have been more divergent. When we came together and tried to reconcile our differences, the process was often less than peaceful. We needed to practice forgiveness and learn some new methods of conflict resolution. In Larry's family, "conflict resolution" was achieved through big brawls—whoever emerged with the least amount of blood on him was dubbed the victor. By contrast, in my family, we would talk things out and compromise, but whoever didn't get his way would walk away with an attitude—one that lingered. Which is worse: a bloody brawl or a long-lingering attitude? Which one wreaks more destruction? I'm not even sure. They're about even, in my estimation. When we got married, Larry and I both had to learn better methods—God's methods—of resolving our differences, so that we could become one.

In addition, the Christian fellowship that we were a part of emphasized the sacrifice of self and of family for the sake of the ministry, and it took years for Larry and me to learn to put each other first. Guess what? Thirty-five years later, we're still learning how to do that. Even when we've been married to our soul mate for years and years, the process of two becoming one never quite ends. It's a lifelong journey. On the path of marriage,

> *Even when we've been married to our soul mate for years and years, the process of two becoming one never quite ends. It's a lifelong journey.*

husband and wife will either move further and further apart or move closer and closer together until they are one unit—indistinguishable from each other. The latter concept is how God intended marriage to be.

Basically, the only reason we can speak so boldly about building great marriages—the reason we can claim God's ability to turn things around—is because we have experienced it ourselves. God has taken the traumas we've been through and turned them into a sense of compassion for others—a desire to see them through the same problems.

Blessings Come When We Follow God's Plan

In order to bless us in every area, including our marriage, God has worked out a plan for us—a path that leads us to success in all aspects of life, including our relationships with our spouses. And His plan does not consist in a bunch of dos and don'ts. It's a bunch of "get to's" and "want to's." His plan, which is laid out in the Bible through the law, is really a path that leads us on the shortest route to the highest level of blessings possible. The law is meant to signify the pathway to all goodness and blessings.

When I first accepted Jesus as my Lord and Savior and became a Christian, I didn't just decide to act differently. In my heart, God gave me a whole new set of "want to's." And that's what we want to develop in our children—a desire and a heart to do what's right, so that, when they're older, they will do it on their own. When Larry and I first became Christians, we came out of the world and stopped acting as we had because something changed on the inside. Our desires had been transformed. Instead of denying ourselves the things we had formerly desired, we started saying, "I don't want to do that anymore, God. I want all that You have for me, instead." This is why, if we're going to raise our children God's way and follow His plan for our families, we must have the living Spirit of God in our homes.

When we say no to God and say yes to junk, we're only hurting ourselves and shortchanging our own futures. God loves us immeasurably, and He wants only the best for us. He accepts us the way we are, but—praise God!—He loves us too much to leave us that way. How many of us became perfect the day we said yes to the Lord and accepted Him into our hearts? How many of us have been perfect in the days since then? I'm not talking about perfection. I'm talking about saying, "You know what, Lord? I blew it. I made a mistake. I gave in to temptation. But I want to move forward. I'm not going to make excuses any longer. I'm going to change, through the power of Your total restoration."

Again, the reason Larry and I are so open about the challenges that we faced early in our marriage, with anger and fighting and immaturity, is that we want you to understand that what God did for us, He'll do for you, too! He is a good God who changes us from glory to glory. Larry and I weren't perfect back then, and we're still far from perfect today. But we see where we want to go, and we're determined to move continually in that direction.

Blessings Come When We're Willing to Change

Jesus said that we can't put new wine in old wineskins, or they will burst. (See Matthew 9:17.) When we give our hearts to the Lord, we become new creations. The old person is gone; a new person has been born. (See 2 Corinthians 5:17.) And we continue to grow by renewing our minds through the Word of God, day by day.

Paul sums it up well in Romans 12:2: "*Don't copy the behavior and customs of this world, but let God transform you into a new person by changing the way you think. Then you will learn to know God's will for you, which is good and pleasing and perfect*" (NLT).

> *When we give our hearts to our spouse, the old person is gone, making way for the birth, or formation, of a new "person"—a new couple.*

The same process must occur in a marriage relationship. When we give our hearts to our spouse, the old person is gone, making way for the birth, or formation, of a new "person"— a new couple. When husband and wife renew their minds together, their relationship grows and evolves so that it resembles more and more closely the relationship of Christ to His bride, the church. (See, for example, Ephesians 5:25–27.)

God's will for us—His plans and purposes for our lives—are always good! He loves us with an infinite, never-ending love, and He wants the absolute best for us. We can trust Him with our eternity, and we can trust Him with our lives while we are on this earth!

Larry and I really do strive to build relationship and our family according to the Word of God. We know and we teach that the Lord is never pointing a finger of accusation at us but is always reaching out a hand to help us. If we will develop a sensitive, repentant heart and merely say, "I admit that I blew it. Forgive me, Lord, for being angry and crabby. Please make me a better person tomorrow, and please renew my mind so that I became more and more like You," it makes a big difference.

Yet, some people just want to dig their heels in and say, "This is the way I am, and nobody's going to change me." The Word of God does a great job of getting past the symptoms and getting to the cause. The Bible says that the Word of God is sharper than any two-edged sword (see Hebrews 4:12), and it never fails to get in there and pull out the crud that interferes with our lives and adversely affects the people around us and put us on the right path—the fast track to success and fulfillment. Isn't that good news?

Repentance is not the same as confession. Repentance is like a soul shower. I was raised in the Catholic Church. At my weekly confession, I would say, "Forgive me, Lord, for I have sinned," and then—guess what?—I would spend the week doing the same things, only to confess them again the following week. But true salvation and repentance are different. You're not just saying, "Forgive me, Lord, for doing such and such." You're saying, "Forgive me, Lord, and cleanse my soul. Change me, Lord, so that I don't go back and do the same things again. From this moment forward, I commit never to go back there again. Please give me Your strength and Your equipping to be strong and committed to moving forward into all that You have for me."

The God we serve answers prayers like that. His anointing, or the smearing of His abilities, is not just for Sunday mornings. His anointing goes with us out the church doors and into the world. He smears us with His abilities so that, no matter the temptations and difficulties we face, His moral compass will guide us in the right direction. His strength will enable us to do the right thing and to walk it out. And this is what we want to teach to our children. It's the Master plan, straight from the Mastermind.

A Resource for All Walks of Life

He said:

You may be a newlywed wondering how to start your marriage out on the right path. You may have been married for some time, and you desire to go from good to great. You may be in a marriage that is struggling, and you don't know how to get past the challenges you're facing. You may have gone through a painful divorce and are wondering if there is hope for your future. You may be facing seemingly insurmountable conflicts with your spouse or with your children. Your family might be in need of a minor tune-up or a major overhaul. Or, you may have a wonderful marriage and family, but you know others who still need some help. You may be a parent searching for a way to raise your kids in the *"training and admonition of the Lord"* (Ephesians 6:4)—whether they're six or sixteen.

Regardless of your situation, it's never too early to get your family going down the right path, nor is it ever too late to steer them back to that path. Our God is a God of hope, restoration, and second chances! Somebody once said that the church is like a body shop, with various wrecks in various stages of repair. Our God is in the business of taking every "wreck" of a life and completely renewing and restoring it! As He does this work in our lives, He is never pointing a finger of accusation at us. He is always reaching out a hand to help us!

No matter who you are, where you've been, what stage of life you're in, or how daunting the challenges you're facing, believe me when I say that God has a new beginning for you! With God's help and a little coaching from Tiz and me, what might have seemed impossible is now within reach.

Get Ready for an Incredible Journey!

She said:

The object of this book is to lead you on the exciting journey of life. Whether you are single, married, divorced, or widowed—and whether or not you have children—God has established a pattern for your life, and He wants to use you to extend His mercy, grace, and healing throughout the world. It's a lofty charge, but you're up to the challenge!

Again, the key is to go step-by-step. Together, we will see the burdens and challenges dissolve and disappear as the blessings of God multiply in your life and family! What the Lord has done for us and for so many others, He wants to do for you. Remember that *"nothing is impossible with God"* (Luke 1:37 NIV)! Place your trust in Him as you step onto the path toward bringing in blessings and being a blessing. Whatever the enemy may have stolen from you, God is going to multiply back to you, in an exponentially greater amount. Your best days are still ahead of you!

> *God has established a pattern for your life, and He wants to use you to extend His mercy, grace, and healing throughout the world.*

Points to Ponder and Apply

+ God is the Author of everything, including marriage, and He set out a plan for success in His Word, the Holy Bible.

+ When we enter into marriage, we are to become a "new creation"—two individuals who are at the same time one unit.

+ The key to improving your marriage and family is to move one step at a time. Practice patience as God does a great work in you!

Chapter 2
THE TWO SHALL BECOME ONE

Life has taught us that love does not consist in gazing at each other but in looking outward together in the same direction.
—Antoine de Saint-Exupéry

She said:

A strong family begins with a strong marriage that's centered on the Lord—a union of two people who become "one flesh," according to the declaration God made at the marriage ceremony of the first couple, Adam and Eve: *"Therefore a man shall leave his father and mother and be joined to his wife, and they shall become one flesh"* (Genesis 2:24).

It's truly a miracle watching two married people become one. Have you ever noticed that many couples start to look alike or often finish each other's sentences? Larry and I do that all the time. If he were to shave his goatee, we'd probably look alike. He is, without a doubt, my soul mate—my *bashert*, in Yiddish. And I am, without a doubt, his soul mate. We're getting to be like the elderly couple who sat down to eat their dinner, and, as the wife began to dish out the meat and vegetables, she asked her husband, "Now, which one of us doesn't like broccoli?"

In Search of a Soul Mate

From the time our children were just black-and-white images on a sonogram, we started praying for their future spouses, wherever they were, and asked God to raise up those men or women He had planned for our kids to marry, to divinely arrange for their paths to intersect, and to eventually raise them up with a special destiny as a couple. Even before our son-in-law, Brandin, was being formed in his mother's womb, we were praying for him, though we had no idea who he was. The same goes for our daughter-in-law, Jen. And we continue to pray for the man God has for our youngest daughter, Katie.

He said:

According to ancient Jewish wisdom, when a man and a woman get married in obedience to God, it isn't a union but a *reunion*. What does that mean? In my case, before the foundations of the earth, Tiz and I were joined as one soul. When it was my time to be born, our souls split, and I became my own being, wandering out into the world. When Tiz was born, the same thing happened— she became her own being. But then, when it was time, God brought us together and made the two halves one again. The tradition of lighting candles on *Shabbat* is based on this belief. Our youngest daughter, Katie, has yet to find her *bashert*, and so she lights her candle. Meanwhile, somewhere out in the world, her *bashert* is lighting his candle, or his mother is doing it for him. Some day, in a world of darkness, these two lights will become one.

Shabbat is a time set apart by God for the family, and we have found it to be the start of understanding the true biblical roles God has for men/husbands/ fathers, women/wives/mothers, and children. God really has put into motion His plan for how the family is to operate and be blessed. We will discuss the concept of *Shabbat* in greater detail in a later chapter.

Becoming One

She said:

"Therefore a man shall leave his father and mother and be joined to his wife, and they shall become one flesh" (Genesis 2:24). The Bible makes it sound so simple. Yet becoming *"one flesh"* is a lifelong journey! Saying "I do" takes two seconds, but the wedding vows are just the first of many steps toward becoming one with your spouse.

How does this "two becoming one" work, exactly? It's a process. You start out as two completely different people living two entirely separate lives. Even when you've found your soul mate—your *bashert*—becoming one is not auto- matic. You may be perfect for each other, but it takes some practice to blend your individual melodies into a beautiful harmony. The reason is that even if you're one in soul, you aren't one in your habits. I'm sure that even as you're reading this, images come to mind that represent the differences between husband and wife: he squeezes the toothpaste tube from the top; she squeezes from the bottom. He's always dropping his wet towel on the floor. She never checks to see if the car needs oil. He leaves his dirty dishes on the counter. She borrows his hammer from his tool box and never puts it back. Sound familiar?

In our marriage, for example, Larry holds himself to a high standard of punctuality, and one of his pet peeves is people who are always running late. He feels that arriving late for appointments, meetings, and other engagements—keeping others waiting—is rude. He would rather be one hour early than one minute late. I absolutely agree with him, admittedly more in theory than in actuality. I've been known to run behind schedule or to hold up the show a time or two (or more). If we have plans to be somewhere, and we're running late because of me, I know there is going to be tension during the drive. Over the years, I have really tried to "fix" this little weakness of mine, and Larry has tried to be more flexible.

On the other hand, when Larry drops his dirty clothes right next to the hamper instead of inside it, *bashert* or not, it annoys me. I think in my mind, *How hard is it? Two more inches, and you'd have made it. Practice your shots.* Over the years, he has gotten to be a much better shot! And I have gotten to be a lot less picky about this issue.

On the path of life, husbands and wives have the opportunity to contribute their own strengths to supplement their spouses' weaknesses.

Every marriage has to work through some differences, big and small. It's a lifelong process. In our sessions of counseling married couples, we hear a lot of "She does this" and "He does this," and it often sounds as if the two sides will never meet. The truth is, men and women are different in many ways. So, the two halves make a whole. She functions this way; he functions that way. These are her strong points; those are his strong points. The key is not to *compete with* each other but to *complete* each other.

Supplement Each Other's Strengths

I was leafing through one of Larry's hunting magazines one day when a headline caught my eye—it said something like, "Why Couples Make Good Hunting Partners." Intrigued, I started reading the article. The author pointed out that men see the big picture, while women are more likely to notice details along the path, and so the two make an excellent team. That's good news! On the path of life, husbands and wives have the opportunity to contribute their own strengths to supplement their spouses' weaknesses.

One of my weaknesses is reading maps. Whenever we travel, we're almost certain to get lost if I'm the navigator. I am "navigationally challenged." If Larry gets frustrated with my navigation skills (or lack thereof), I simply remind him about the article in his hunting magazine. I tell him, "You have your strengths, and I have mine. We have to cover for each other!" If we view our differences from a perspective of competition, we end up frustrated with each other. But if we view them as completion—two sets of strengths that come together to make a whole—we end up appreciating one another. (At least, that's the way it's supposed to work!)

In our marriage, Larry is the big-picture person. He's the visionary. I, on the other hand, am the detail person. I like to say, "He's the headlines; I'm the fine print." He lays out the vision and chases after it, while I take care of the details to make it happen. He doesn't want my job, and I don't want his, because we aren't gifted in the same way. That's why, together, we make a great team.

Having said all that, I do want to add that there are a lot of minor annoyances things that can quickly turn into major irritations. A good marriage develops when we each genuinely try to work through these differences or irritations and determine not to make a mountain out of a molehill.

He said:

The idea that men and women should have complementary qualities was hatched in the garden of Eden, and we see it in the subtleties of the creation narrative. Throughout the first and second chapters of Genesis, God has been creating the earth, the plants, the animals, and so forth. Seven times, He says, "It is good"—the earth is good, the lakes are good, the animals are good, and so on. Everything has been positive so far.

But then, God identifies something that isn't good: *"And the LORD God said, 'It is not good that man should be alone'"* (Genesis 2:18). This doesn't apply just to men, of course—it isn't good for anybody to be alone! Still, it's worth noting that those who get into the most trouble with the law are single men. Those who cause the most problems, whether by stealing, hurting, murdering, or another manner, are, by far, single males. When God said that it is not good for man to be alone, He wasn't saying, "Men, it isn't good for you to be without a woman."

My friend Rabbi Lapin tells a great story to illustrate this truth. Let's say you're walking down a dark alley around one o'clock in the morning. (My first question is, what are you doing in an alley at one o'clock in the morning?) All of a sudden, you see six people walking your way, and your heart starts to beat faster and faster. *What are these guys going to do?* you ask yourself. But then, when they get closer, you can see that there are three men and three women. At that point, your anxiety decreases significantly. Why? Because the presence of a woman changes a man. If there aren't any women around, men act differently.

To remedy Adam's aloneness, God came up with a solution: *"I will make him a helper comparable to him"* (Genesis 2:18). The word *"comparable"* is actually a poor translation. A better translation from the Hebrew is "opposite to him." Why is that fitting? Because the world depends on opposites binding together—on complementary elements functioning in their roles to achieve a specific result. For example, water consists in a bound between hydrogen and oxygen. Air consists in oxygen, nitrogen, and other trace elements binding together. Salt is composed of sodium and chlorine—two elements that are poisonous by themselves!

> *Opposites bound by God result in miracles.*

The analogy gets even better. Not only are these elements bound together—a miracle of God in and of itself—but, singularly, by themselves, they bring destruction; they poison. Yet, combined with other elements, they constitute something phenomenal and life-giving.

Going back to Genesis 2:18, we see that it made sense for God to create a helper "opposite to" man. This is why men don't marry men, women don't marry women, brothers don't marry sisters, and so forth. An opposite is what you want. If you have too much of the same substance, it can combust and cause an explosion. But opposites bound by God result in miracles.

Let's read on. You might expect the following verses to describe the creation of this helper "opposite" of Adam, but no. God had a special plan for creating Eve, as we will see.

Verses 19–20 read as follows:

Out of the ground the Lord God formed every beast of the field and every bird of the air, and brought them to Adam to see what he would call them. And whatever Adam called each living creature, that was its name. So Adam gave names to all cattle, to the birds of the air, and to every beast of the field. But for Adam there was not found a helper comparable to him.

Now, why is it that what follows God's proclamation "It isn't good for man to be alone" is Adam's naming of the animals? God brought each animal before Adam, and he said, "Giraffe...nope, too tall for me." "Hippopotamus...a little too wide." There's a reason that man cannot live properly without his "opposite." None of the animals was suitable. Adam could have said, "Well, I don't need anybody; I've got God." But God said, "That's not enough."

So, God created a helper for Adam.

And the LORD God caused a deep sleep to fall on Adam, and he slept; and He took one of his ribs, and closed up the flesh in its place. Then the rib which the LORD God had taken from man He made into a woman, and He brought her to the man. And Adam said: "This is now bone of my bones and flesh of my flesh; she shall be called Woman, because she was taken out of Man."

(Genesis 2:21–23)

I am not suggesting that everybody run out and get married. Those who are married know that no one and nothing can complete us as God does, and, after that, there is a need that He fills by bringing an "opposite" into our lives.

Give Up to Go Up

She said:

In Matthew 9:17, Jesus explained that new wine cannot be contained in old wineskins. In other words, the old, used vessels could not contain the spiritual freshness and explosive growth of the "new wine," or spiritual freshness. In the same way, when we get married, we have to change and renew certain aspects of life to make room for the new growth and exciting adventures ahead of us. Inflexibility, resistance to change, and remaining stuck in our old ways often hinder us from embracing the new phase that marriage brings to our lives. In order to prevent these issues from causing problems, it's often helpful to "give up to go up."

The process of "two becoming one" sometimes requires some lifestyle adaptations and initial sacrifice. You will likely find that some things are no longer compatible with your lifestyle once you get married. Sometimes, old relationships, old activities, and old hangouts simply aren't conducive to strengthening the marriage relationship. But the initial sacrifice is minor compared to the payoff in building your lifelong bond with your spouse.

When Larry and I got married, I was twenty-one years old. Growing up in Montana, my favorite pastimes were snow skiing and waterskiing, neither of which Larry had ever attempted. I decided that I would rather be with him and find common hobbies we could enjoy together. Before long, camping and hiking became some of our favorite things to do as a couple and, later, as a family of five. A few years after we got married, Larry took up skiing, so we were able to add that to the list of things we enjoyed doing together.

Sometimes, it's wise to give up certain pastimes, at least for a season, in order to build a deeper bond with your spouse. I have counseled many couples and found that an unwillingness to forfeit something or someone for the sake of the marriage can take a severe toll on the relationship.

Jesus said, *"He who finds his life will lose it, and he who loses his life for My sake will find it"* (Matthew 10:39). I believe that this verse can be applied to our marriages. Here is a request God will honor without fail: "God, I'm going to let go of some things that mean something to me, but I believe that as I redirect that effort and energy toward our marriage, You're going to multiply the blessings back to me."

The primary reason for giving up certain activities and friendships is to make room for new interests you and your spouse can enjoy together. It doesn't mean that you have to compromise your identity; it just means that you are evolving into a couple. This is a course that will bring enormous growth and enjoyment to you throughout the course of your marriage.

I like to compare a marriage to a bank account. If you go to the bank to make a withdrawal, you can withdraw only as much as the amount you have invested. A big deposit yields big returns.

> *The investment of sacrifice for the sake of intimacy will yield major returns in the long run.*

Marriage works the same way: you get out of it only what you have invested into it. And the investment of sacrifice for the sake of intimacy will yield major returns in the long run.

Becoming one with your spouse requires that you travel on the same course. If your spouse is going one way while you're going another, you somehow need to make your paths converge. And, again, this often requires that you give up something. I'm not saying that you can't keep up with your old friends or pursue certain activities on your own—just don't allow those activities to consume all your time or your energy. Don't allow them to engulf your life to the point where your spouse is bumped to the bottom of your priorities list. Otherwise, you'll end up giving your best to other people and having only scrappy little leftovers for your own spouse. You cannot sustain a strong marriage that way! I have seen too many marriages drift further and further apart because of separate activities and friends. Statistics show that the most common scenario for infidelity taking place is hanging out at the wrong places with the wrong people. A good safeguard is this: Don't go looking for something in other people or other places that you're missing at home. It takes effort top build a strong marriage relationship, but I promise you that it's well worth the effort!

As you give up some of the activities you used to enjoy before getting married, it makes room for the addition of new activities you can enjoy with your spouse. Our son, Luke, and his wife, Jen, both love to barbecue. When they got married, they went out and bought a little barbecue grill for cooking on together. It's cute to hear them compare the recipes they've researched as they talk about what they're going to make next.

Submission: A Separate but Equal Task

He said:

Wives, likewise, be submissive to your own husbands, that even if some do not obey the word, they, without a word, may be won by the conduct of their wives, when they observe your chaste conduct accompanied by fear. Do not let your adornment be merely outward; arranging the hair, wearing gold, or putting on fine apparel; rather let it be the hidden person of the heart, with the incorruptible beauty of a gentle and quiet spirit, which is very precious in the sight of God. For in this manner, in former times, the holy women who trusted in God also adorned themselves, being submissive to their own husbands, as Sarah obeyed Abraham, calling him lord, whose daughters you are if you do good and are not afraid with any terror. Husbands, likewise, dwell with them with understanding, giving honor to the wife, as to the weaker vessel, and as being heirs together of the grace of life, that your prayers may not be hindered.

(1 Peter 3:1–7)

Wives, submit to your own husbands, as to the Lord. For the husband is head of the wife, as also Christ is head of the church; and He is the Savior of the body. Therefore, just as the church is subject to Christ, so let the wives be to their own husbands in everything. Husbands, love your wives, just as Christ also loved the church and gave Himself for her, that He might sanctify and cleanse her with the washing of water by the word, that He might present her to Himself a glorious church, not having spot or wrinkle or any such thing, but that she should be holy and without blemish. So husbands ought to love their own wives as their own bodies; he who loves his wife loves himself. For no one ever hated his own flesh, but nourishes and cherishes it, just as the Lord does the church. For we are members of His body, of His flesh and of His bones. "For this reason a man shall leave his father and mother and be joined to his wife, and the two shall become one flesh." (Ephesians 5:22–31)

In the above passages, we see the pattern God established for marriage. It's sobering to think that the degree to which we function according to His design determines whether He hears our prayers. (See 1 Peter 3:7.) We may be children of God who love Him and His Word, but if we reject our roles as husbands and wives, He says, "I can't hear your prayers." Sobering, isn't it?

Now, these passages tend to make a lot of people uncomfortable because they deal with submission. And I'll admit that in all of my years of pastoring, I've realized that even husbands who know next to nothing about the Bible are familiar with one Scripture: *"Wives, submit to your own husbands"* (Ephesians 5:22). It's amazing—they couldn't find the book of Genesis if you paid them, but they know this one thing: "Wife, I'm the man, and you are to submit to me."

But we need to make sure we get the whole picture. Later on in the same passage from Ephesians, it says, *"Husbands, love your wives, just as Christ also loved the church and gave Himself for her"* (verse 25). Husbands, before your wife submits to you, there's a requirement you must meet: you are to love your wife as Christ loves the church. In other words, you need to be committed enough to your wife that you would die for her. You also need to model Christ's love for the church in how you treat your wife.

A husband has three primary roles to fulfill in relation to his wife and family: (1) sanctification, (2) provision, and (3) protection. Yet these duties do not make him superior to his wife or give him the right to rule or dominate her, since each of them has a corresponding quality she possesses in greater measure than he.

1. Sanctification

> *Husbands, love your wives, just as Christ also loved the church and gave Himself for her, that He might sanctify and cleanse her with the washing of water by the word, that He might present her to Himself a glorious church, not having spot or wrinkle or any such thing, but that she should be holy and without blemish.*   (Ephesians 5:25–27, emphasis added)

The reason why so many women have a problem with the biblical command "Wives, submit to your husbands" is the same reason so many people have a problem with the word "law" when it comes to the Scriptures. They don't know what it really means in context. God's "laws" are not just a big list of restrictions. Ancient Hebrew teaches us that the word for "law" literally means "the path"—the path to all of God's incredible blessings! Remember, God is not a taker; He is a giver!

> *If a man refuses to submit to Jesus Christ, then his wife is not obligated to submit to him, because he is disqualified to be an authority in her life, as well as in his household.*

We tend to think we know what it is to "submit"—man's in charge, and woman must do whatever he says. The word has a negative connotation and automatically ruffles feathers. So, let's back up a few verses. Ephesians 5:23 reminds us that *"the husband is head of the wife, as also Christ is head of the church."* And in 1 Corinthians 11:3, we read, *"The head of every man is Christ, the head of woman is man, and the head of Christ is God."* Clearly, women aren't the only ones who are to submit. Men must submit to Christ, who is their ultimate spiritual authority. If a man refuses to submit to Jesus Christ, then his wife is not obligated to submit to him, because he is disqualified to be an authority in her life, as well as in his household.

It is only by mutual submission that men and women are sanctified—made to be like Christ, without spot or blemish. Men, if you want this "submission" thing to work, you need to come to church and to submit yourselves to the lordship of Jesus Christ. You can't simply send your wives and children to church. That's like preaching one thing but practicing another. So, men, you must begin serving God.

We still need to understand what Paul meant by the word "submit." Contrary to a common assumption, submission does not imply a state of inequality, with one party being superior to the other. Man and woman were created equal, just as pastors and laypeople are created equal. My position as pastor of a church does not make me superior to my congregation. In fact, it means that I am entrusted with the job of serving my congregation. It doesn't make me better or superior or give me the right to dominate or abuse them.

The same thing is true in the home. While the wife is to submit to her husband, the husband is to serve his wife and also to sanctify her. That's what the Bible means when it says, *"Wives, submit…as to the Lord."* "To submit" does not mean "to be subservient to." In Hebrew, the word for *submit* means "to care for" or "to recognize." By "submitting" to the Lord, we recognize Him for who He is; we also "care for" Him through worship, tithing, and so on. We are not fearful of or subservient to Him. We're joint-heirs with His Son, Jesus, remember? (See Romans 8:16–17.) So, we pray to Him, we study His Word, we pray, we give our tithes and offerings, and we obey Him. We worship Him, because the Lord has said, "If My people won't praise Me, I'll call upon the rocks and stones to praise Me, instead." (See Luke 19:40.) The word for "praise" in that verse is the same word for "submit"; it means recognizing someone's identity and caring for that person. In a nutshell, it really comes down to honor and respect, which is what we all want.

She said:

So often, when women hear the term "submit," they automatically cringe and get defensive. I think Larry has done a great job of teaching on what this term really means, but I would like to add a woman's point of view. I come from a long line of strong, independent, hardworking, business-minded women. I was twenty when I became a Christian, and I distinctly remember the first time I heard my pastor preach on the family and say that a wife was to submit to her husband. I remember thinking, *What in the world have I gotten myself into? This is not going to work for me!* Keep in mind that this was in the 1970s, when the Women's Liberation Movement was at its peak. I nearly walked out of the church and never came back!

After the service, I sought out my pastor's wife and asked her to explain this "submission thing" to me. She laughed and said, "I understand how you are feeling! Don't worry; this is a good thing!" She then explained briefly that the term "submit" didn't mean "to be subservient" or "to be dominated." It really is all about God's order. She explained to me that a husband is to honor, respect, love, protect, and cover his wife. To illustrate the concept of being "covered by" a husband, she told me to picture a garage where a car is kept. A woman who is covered by her husband is like a car you pull into a garage to protect and shelter it from a storm.

A wife is to honor, respect, love, and submit—or yield—to her husband, the same way that we all are to submit, or yield, to the Lord. My pastor's wife gave me another illustration that was tremendously helpful to my understanding. The term "submit" essentially means "to adapt," "to join," or "to merge." At that point, it clicked for me! I tried to picture two completely separate, independent people getting married and then continuing to move along two separate paths of life, neither one willing to "merge" his or her path with the other's. If this pattern continues, the husband and wife will never really join their lives together as one. In fact, the two paths will probably get further and further apart as time goes on. So, a wife's willingness to merge her life, her dreams, and her future with her husband's—to join her path with his—is not giving up her identity, talents, or potential. Rather, the two become one, and each of them receives a more complete identity that contributes to a fabulous family that lasts forever!

He said:

2. Protection

The name of the Lord *is a strong tower; the righteous run to it and are safe.*
(Proverbs 18:10)

"No weapon formed against you shall prosper, and every tongue which rises against you in judgment You shall condemn. This is the heritage of the servants of the Lord, *and their righteousness is from Me," says the* Lord.
(Isaiah 54:17)

A primary tendency of a man's nature is to protect, while a primary tendency of a woman's nature is to nurture. In Judaism, these roles are separate but equal. I can give you a great example. Many years ago, our family took hike in the woods. Tiz was walking with Katie, who was about three years old, and holding her hand. Luke and Anna, who were around seven and ten years old at the time, were about thirty yards ahead of us on the trail. We lost sight of them for just a moment when they went around a bend. And then, wouldn't you know it, a bear came out of the woods! Do you think Tiz said, "Stand back, Larry! I'll handle the bear"? No! Without even thinking, she practically threw me at the bear. She pushed me forward, putting me between her and Katie and the bear.

Why? Because she is a nurturer, while I am a protector. It wasn't a matter of my being better than she or more qualified to fight off the bear; it was simply that her role was to nurture, while mine was to protect—separate yet equal duties. So, Tiz "submitted" to me by recognizing my duty to protect her. It wasn't Tiz's nature to confront that bear. It was her instinct to protect her baby.

If something goes bump in the middle of the night, it's rare for a husband to wake up and say, "Honey, I think I heard a noise." Usually, the wife hears the noise, wakes up her husband, and refuses to go back to sleep until he checks it out.

In rabbinical literature, the word for the submissive spirit—the nurturing, caring attitude—is actually considered more important than the protective spirit. We know that Jesus protects us, but we also know that He cares for us, and that is an ongoing state, as opposed to the case-by-case basis of protection. Jewish rabbis teach that the reason why this is sometimes more important is that, in the creation account in Genesis, the Bible says that man was "made," or "formed," while the woman was "built." In other words, man was formed, but woman was built to certain specifications. The Hebrew word that means "to build" is *banah*, which implies that the woman was created with a deeper sense of intuition, understanding, and intelligence. It's a woman who makes a house a home. She builds the nest, while the man defends it by fighting off the enemy.

3. Provision

> *The LORD will open to you His good treasure, the heavens, to give the rain to your land in its season, and to bless all the work of your hand. You shall lend to many nations, but you shall not borrow.* (Deuteronomy 28:12)

> *Therefore do not worry, saying, "What shall we eat?" or "What shall we drink?" or "What shall we wear?" For after all these things the Gentiles seek. For your heavenly Father knows that you need all these things. But seek first the kingdom of God and His righteousness, and all these things shall be added to you.* (Matthew 6:31–33)

> *My God shall supply all your need according to His riches in glory by Christ Jesus.* (Philippians 4:19)

The Bible says, "*But if anyone does not provide for his own, and especially for those of his household, he has denied the faith and is worse than an unbeliever*" (1 Timothy 5:8). In the King James Version, this same verse labels a man who fails to provide for his family *"worse than an infidel."* Ouch! I want you to think about that. I'm not picking on anybody, but if a man is a child of God and he fails to work a job to provide for his wife and children, in God's eyes, he is worse than an unbeliever.

Of course, women have the right to earn a living and build a career, if they want to. Consider the "Proverbs 31" woman—she is extremely industrious, making linen garments to sell. (See verse 24.) Tiz's mother had a career and worked full-time, on top of her duties as a full-time mom. Similarly, Tiz has always been involved in full-time ministry, in addition to being a wonderful wife and mom full-time. And for most of our married life, we have had other businesses to which she has devoted significant amounts of time and energy. This has been our choice over the years. Whether a wife and mom chooses to work is a matter of choice and/or circumstances. But it's up to Mom whether she stays at home or works elsewhere.

> *If you are a man, and you are physically and mentally capable of work, your job is to provide for your family.*

With the man, however, there is no choice. God never intended for there to be "stay-at-home dads." Granted, there are exceptions, such as when someone is unable to work due to physical limitations or other extenuating circumstances. But, if you are a man, and you are physically and mentally capable of work, your job is to provide for your family. As a matter of fact, the Bible says, *"If anyone will not work, neither shall he eat"* (2 Thessalonians 3:10).

Now, I thank God that we live in a country that has programs to help people in need. But if we're accepting welfare when we could be working a job, that's not having a need met; that's stealing. One of the most spiritual things a man can do is to work a job. In describing male leaders, the Bible almost always lists their occupations prior to becoming disciples or apostles or prophets. These men were diligent workers and faithful providers.

Let me help you, ladies. If you're looking to get married, look for a man who's serving God and working a job. I like to tell the following joke to illustrate this point. An American and an Englishman are traveling on a train, and the Englishman says to the American, "I say, my good man, are there any gentlemen in America?" The American replies, "What do you mean by 'gentlemen'?" The Englishman says, "A gentleman, sir, is someone who does not work for a living." The American replies, "Oh, sure, we've got plenty of those, but we call them 'bums'!"

I have prayed for too many men who have said something along the lines of, "I've been out of work for several years." Under normal circumstances, that should never be the case. If you've been out of work for a significant length of time, maybe you need to consider taking a job that you consider "beneath you," for the time being. If the ideal job isn't available, we need to be willing to do whatever it takes to support our families. Sometimes—no offense to anyone—it's a simple case of laziness.

The Bible says that God will bless everything you put your hands to. (See, for example, Deuteronomy 28:8.) It doesn't say that He will bless anything you put your backside to, so get up off the couch and go get a job! You may say, "I'm trusting in the Lord to meet my needs." That's fine—trust in the Lord while you're digging a ditch! Welfare is for people who can't work, not people who won't work.

Love and Respect—Two Sides of the Same Coin

The apostle Paul concluded his comments on marriage in Ephesians 5 with the following exhortation: *"Nevertheless let each one of you in particular so love his own wife as himself, and let the wife see that she respects her husband"* (verse 33). In our marriages—in the process of two becoming one—there has to be mutual self-sacrifice and mutual contribution. And here is where we often get into trouble. God says to the husband, "Love your wife," and the husband replies, "How can I love her when she doesn't respect me?" God says to the wife, "Respect your husband," and the wife replies, "How can I respect him when he doesn't love me?"

Be Mature

As my mother often told me, "Someday, you're going to have to grow up." The problem is that there are too many forty-, fifty-, and sixty-year-old kids. Most of us are familiar with the squabbles of kids in the backseat of a car: "Mom, he's touching me again!" "No, I'm not!" "You kids stop that, or I'm going to turn this car around." "Mom, he's doing it again!" Have you ever seen adults acting like that? Of course, you have. Somebody needs to grow up first. Wives, stop poking your husband. Husbands, stop poking your wife. Otherwise, God's going to turn this car around.

"He started it!" "No, she started it!" It doesn't matter who started it—both of you, stop it! Let's be mature enough to decide to put an end to the vicious, downward cycle of bickering and blaming. And then, let's make a point to begin a powerful, upward cycle! Nothing eats away at your marriage more drastically than disrespectful, demeaning treatment of each other. Mutual respect, appreciation, and kindness are to a marriage what oil, grease, and gasoline are to an automobile. If your car runs out of these things, you're going to get stuck somewhere or blow up your engine. If your marriage runs out of these things…you get the picture! As with our cars, it's much better to keep up with the maintenance than to deal with the consequences of failing to do so.

Affirm Your Spouse with Love and Respect

Men, before your wife shows you respect, start loving her as Christ loved the church. And don't belittle your wife, either. It may be that her primary need is love, but that doesn't negate her need of respect. One of the worst things you can do to your wife, if she's a stay-at-home mom, is to come back from work and say to her, "What have you done all day?" I honestly do not know how mothers raise their kids without the help of their families. Don't be stupid, men. Don't ever say, "What have you done all day?" Her job starts before you even wake up and goes on long aver you've gone to bed. It's a never-ending job. And, women, before your husband shows you love, start respecting him as God respects you, even if he doesn't have a job.

In marriage, our goal should always be to encourage our spouse through positive words, loyalty, appreciation, and other shows of support.

As you know, Tiz and I have been married and doing ministry together for thirty-five years. Every Sunday afternoon of those years, as Tiz and I have gotten in our car to drive home after the morning services, the first words out of Tiz's mouth have been something like this: "What a great service!" "That message was powerful!" "That message touched so many people!" Now, surely, in thirty-five years of preaching, there must have been a time or two when my message was less than stellar. If that was the case, I never heard it from Tiz! I'm not denying the value of constructive criticism, but—let's be honest—the world dishes out plenty of that. In marriage, our goal should always be to encourage our spouse through positive words, loyalty, appreciation, and other shows of support. It's like a boomerang: what we "throw" at our spouses comes back to us. Let's make a concentrated effort to build up our spouses, not to tear them down.

Points to Ponder and Apply

+ Men and women are different by design, with the purpose of completing each other, not competing with each other.

+ A woman brings out unique qualities in a man, which is one reason God said that it wasn't good for man to be alone.

+ The three primary duties of a man, in regard to his wife and family, are (1) sanctification, (2) provision, and (3) protection.

+ The process of "two becoming one" will require some changes, major and minor. As you "give up to go up," look for new activities you can enjoy together.

+ A husband who expects his wife to submit to him must meet God's requirements: (1) submit to God, and (2) love his wife as Christ loves the church.

Chapter 3
BACK TO EDEN: WE AREN'T ANIMALS

*Adam and Eve had an ideal marriage. He didn't have to hear about
all the men she could have married, and she didn't have to hear
about how well his mother cooked.*
—Author Unknown

He said:

In the previous chapter, we talked about husbands and wives being separate but equal in marriage. Let's talk now about how that came to be. It all started back in the garden of Eden. But there are nuances that will bring a tremendous revelation for you, as well. The rules haven't changed, and we need to understand the clues that are concealed for us in the creation account.

Be a Man, Not a Male

When God created man, He called him "Adam," which comes from the Hebrew word *adomis*, meaning "from the earth" or "from the ground": *"You will return to the ground from which you came. For you were made from the ground, and to the ground you will return"* (Genesis 3:19 TLB). *Adomis* refers to mankind—males and females. Therefore, God created both male and female in His image, and the two are equal in the eyes of God.

Again, though our Bibles use the name Adam in Genesis 1 through 3, the translation is "man," because the Latin word for "earth" is *humanus*, from which we get the word "human." So, the Bible isn't talking about male or female; it's talking about human beings, or mankind as a whole.

It Takes a Woman to Make a Male a Man

Now, look at Genesis 2:22. We read that the rib was taken from *"man"*— natural man, a human being, a part of nature. Adam was just like any other male in the created order. But, the moment the woman comes on the scene, everything changes. The Hebrew word for "woman" is *'ishah*, and it doesn't just mean "female." It also means "wife" and "mother." So, up until this point, God was talking about human nature in Adam, and then, all of a sudden, He creates woman, Eve, and calls her *'ishah*—wife and mother. Watch what happens. Adam calls Eve "*bone of my bones and flesh of my flesh; she shall be called Woman ['ishah], because she was taken out of Man ['ish]*" (Genesis 2:23). Up until this point, "Adam" simply referred to mankind, a part of nature. But, starting with the creation of Eve, or *'ishah*—which means "wife" and "mother"—Adam is called *'ish*—"husband" and "father." What accounts for the shift in terminology? It's like we said in the previous chapter: the presence of a woman changes a man. The reason why Adam, the male, was changed the moment his wife came on the scene is because he had been preparing a home for her.

It Takes a Responsible Man to Earn a Woman's Respect

When Eve came into the world, Adam had everything ready. He'd been tilling the garden God had planted him in. Prior to the creation of man, the earth took care of itself: "*Before any plant of the field was in the earth and before any herb of the field had grown. For the LORD God had not caused it to rain on the earth, and there was no man to till the ground; but a mist went up from the earth and watered the whole face of the ground*" (Genesis 2:5–6). Nature cares about itself, but you need two opposites working together to create a home. And so, before the creation of Eve, Adam was preparing for her coming. She was immediately placed in an environment that Adam had prepared to welcome her—a home with provisions. The word *'ish* means "husband," but, in a deeper sense, it also means "provider," "protector," "one who is considerate," and "one who is caring." The moment Eve was created, she felt immediate respect for Adam because he was already providing for her. He had been preparing for her. He learned to be emotionally open with her and to treat her with affection.

> The moment Eve was created, she felt immediate respect for Adam because he was already providing for her.

He was also kind to her. At times, it seems as if we've forgotten how to be kind to each other in the home. We give "common courtesy" to the outside world but fail to make it a common practice in our own homes. This should not be.

So, Eve was birthed as a woman/wife, and she had immediate respect for her husband because he had been working hard to prepare for her arrival. Let me give you an illustration. At the wedding ceremony, who is standing at the altar waiting? The man. Who is coming down the aisle? The woman. Why? It's a reenactment of what happened in the garden of Eden. The moment Eve came on the scene, Adam was ready. He'd worked the garden and gotten everything prepared for her.

You are probably familiar with the passage where Paul says, "Wives, honor and respect your husbands; husbands, love your wives." (See Ephesians 5:22–28.) And that ought to happen. But if it were really happening in the church, divorces among Christian couples would not outnumber divorce in the secular world. We're missing something. And here's just one part of the problem: husbands, you can't simply command your wives to honor you on the basis of your being males. If you're acting like an animal, you can't expect her to respect or honor you.

Similarly, wives, you can't simply command your husbands to love you just because you're females if you're acting like animals. There are a lot of men who have never grown up. They may be fifty-something; they may be males; but they aren't men. Men work a job. Men earn a steady income. Any male can get married and produce offspring, but that doesn't make him an *'ish*. Respect is the natural response of a woman when her husband works a job, pays the bills, acts responsibly, and treats his family with love and kindness. If your wife stops respecting you, maybe something is out of line with God's plan.

This is why, whenever we have marriage preparation classes, we tell the women, "Don't marry a bum." Don't even date a bum. Just because he's a male doesn't make him a good candidate for a husband. He needs to be working a job, serving the Lord, paying his debts on time, and taking care of business. You also shouldn't expect to change him once you're married. He is as good as he'll ever be while he's wooing you. It's not all that different from animals in mating season: the males puff up their feathers to impress the females.

The moment Eve was created, she was an *'ishah*. She was a woman and a wife—yes, she was a female—but she had this other, special quality within her. It's within a woman to honor her husband. But the husband has to be one who works a job and pays his bills and goes to church and leads his family and cares for them. He can't just command his wife to honor him and show him respect. He has to earn her respect by being not just "Adam," a man, but an *'ish*—a man of God.

Be a Man, Not an Animal

Genesis chapter 1 gives an account of creation that's repeated in Genesis chapter 2, albeit with slightly different wording. And every word is there for a reason. Why is the account of the creation of man and woman related in both of the first two chapters of Genesis? Because everything God does has two components—a physical part and a spiritual part—and, in this case, the account in Genesis 1 is a physical description, while the account in Genesis 2 is more spiritual in significance.

In Genesis 2:7, it says, *"And the* Lord *God formed man of the dust of the ground, and breathed into his nostrils the breath of life; and man became a living being."* Then, in verse 19, it says, *"Out of the ground the* Lord *God formed every beast of the field and every bird of the air, and brought them to Adam to see what he would call them."*

From these verses, we learn that God *"formed"* man and then *"formed"* the animals. In English, the same verb is used for both events. But in the original Hebrew, that wasn't the case. It's hard for us to appreciate, since most people aren't familiar with the Hebrew language, but the word for *"formed"* is different depending on whether it applies to mankind or to animals. When God *"formed"* man, the word that's used is different from the verb that's used to say, for example, that He *"formed"* a cow. The distinction is minute—it comes down to one little jot, which is the smallest type of character in the Hebrew language.

> *Even though we humans were created to inhabit the same world as animals, we were not designed to act like they do.*

What's the significance, you ask? It points to the difference in what was formed. Whether you're a man or a woman, you're not an animal, so you shouldn't act like one. Animals were not filled with the breath of God, as humans were. Therefore, even though we humans were created to inhabit the same world as animals, we were not designed to act like they do. Animals can't help the way they are. They act on instinct and aren't equipped with a conscience, so they'll kill one another without a second thought and won't be held morally responsible for their actions.

A Man Does Not Follow His Primal Instincts

Animals basically live by the motto "If it feels good, do it." Animals can't help it, because they don't have the Spirit of God in them. They put themselves first because it's instinctual. A male lion isn't chivalrous; he's going to eat before the females and the cubs. Even if it means that his offspring will die of starvation, he's going to eat.

I have a few horses. When it's feeding time, those horses will kick each other in their attempts to be first to the feeding trough. They can't help it. You can't tell a hungry bear, "Don't act like that!"

Here is another example of how animals differ from humans—or ought to. In most states, it's illegal to hunt an animal during its mating season. Why? Because it isn't fair to the animals. When it's breeding season, they aren't thinking straight. You hear stories of moose standing in the middle of the tracks when a train is coming. That's the animal world.

But we aren't animals—we are children of God, formed in His image. We can control our urges. We can't say, "Well, I cheated on my wife; I couldn't help it." That would be a lie. "Well, everybody else is doing it." It doesn't matter. Each of us is a child of God, and God has breathed His breath in our nostrils, not the animals'. We are not to follow the ways of nature. If God tells us not to do something, then we don't do it. We don't act like animals. We don't fornicate like animals; we don't steal like animals; we don't fight like animals.

A Man Does Not Deny His Wrongdoing

After Adam and Eve had eaten the fruit from the forbidden tree, they were thrown out of the garden. (See Genesis 3:22–24.) Both of them had sinned, and both were spiritually divorced from God, in a manner of speaking. Sometimes, separation from God occurs because of something the woman did. In this case, however, it was the fault of the man. In Hebrew tradition, it's the man who makes or breaks a marriage. If a marriage goes south, most of the time, the man is to blame. Sure, there are some women who are bad news. But, most of the time, the man is at fault for a failed marriage. He stops being an *'ish* and starts acting like an Adam—a typical male in the world.

Now, in the garden, Eve was at fault, too. But in general, the man is at fault 95 percent of the time. Men, if our marriages don't work, it's because we're either bad pickers or bad husbands. In marriage counseling sessions, the men almost always say, "I picked wrong." But if we become the men God wants us to be, then our wives will honor us.

Let's return to Adam and Eve. In Genesis 4:1, we read, *"Now Adam knew Eve his wife, and she conceived and bore Cain, and said, 'I have acquired a man from the* LORD.'" Does her comment strike you as a little strange? When was the last time you received a birth announcement that said, "It's a man!"?

Eve wasn't speaking under the influence of an epidural used to soothe her birthing pains. Her declaration actually had two meanings—and neither of them pertained to her baby boy! Let's see how this works.

Eve's husband, Adam, had disobeyed God, eaten from the tree, and forfeited the life he and his wife had enjoyed in the garden of Eden. So, to make up for his mistake, he decided to get right with God by obeying Him, for once, starting with the command to *"be fruitful and multiply"* (Genesis 1:28). Adam said to Eve, "We need to start obeying God. Let's have a baby." And so, he "knew" Eve, who conceived, bore Cain, and said, "I have gotten a man from the Lord." Now, you might presume that she was merely declaring the sex of her baby. Not so. The word for *"man"* here is not *Adomis* but *'ish*—"husband." She was saying, "I've gotten a *husband* from the Lord." And this seemingly simple acknowledgment must have touched the heart of Adam. She was saying, in essence, "My husband blew it and got us kicked out of paradise, but now he's gotten his heart right, and I can say once more that I have a husband who comes from the Lord."

A Man Assumes Responsibility for His Decisions

Let me show you the second thing Eve meant when she said, "I have a husband from the Lord." Pregnancy and childbirth effect tremendous change on a woman because it's no longer just her own safety she's concerned with. From the minute she knows she's pregnant, her concern shifts to the tasks of caring for, sheltering, feeding, and protecting her baby.

In the animal world, it's the same way. But female animals need to be even more protective, because all the males care about is sex. Lions, tigers, bears—all they want is sex. They don't care about their offspring. In many cases, the moment the female gives birth, she does everything in her power to keep her young away from the male who fathered them, because she knows he might kill them and eat them just to have sex with her again.

It doesn't take a spiritual man to fornicate. It doesn't require any anointing to sleep together. Animals do it all the time. But we're not animals!

When a mother has a baby—whether she's a human, a bear, an eagle, or a dolphin—her first priority is to tend to her child. In the animal kingdom, the male usually goes his own way, but the female spends all of her energy caring for her young. And so, when Eve saw how much love her husband, Adam, had for their child, and when she realized that he wasn't the type to get a girl pregnant and then run off, never to be heard from again, she said, "I have an 'ish—a husband, a man of God." A man who does not neglect his wife and children is saying, "I'm not an animal. I'm not just going to breed and then run off, never to return. I'm going to take care of my children, because it's my ministry."

The number one sign in Judaism of being under a curse is a son who doesn't know who his father is. Recall that when Joseph was in a position of leadership in Egypt, and his brothers came to seek relief from the famine, they didn't recognize him, and so he asked them, "Do you have a father? Is he still alive?" (See Genesis 43:27.) What he meant by these questions was, "Do you have a relationship with your dad?" The difference between us humans and the animals is that if we have kids, we need to know them. We need to take care of them. Any male can birth a child, but it takes a true man to father a child. We have been formed in the image of God, so we don't just sleep with anybody we want to. We don't fornicate because we feel like it. Until you have a ring on your finger—until you've said "I do"—you don't. Society says, "What difference does a ring make?" A ring is the difference between a blessing and a curse.

> Society says, "What difference does a ring make?" A ring is the difference between a blessing and a curse.

A Man Puts His Family Before Everything Else

There are a lot of husbands who say, "I don't know why my wife is leaving me. I did such and such for her." But if we come home at eleven or twelve o'clock at night—maybe we aren't running around, we're just working late at the office—we have it backward. If we're going to make our families survive and thrive, if we want our wives to honor us, they need to see us loving our kids.

But the husband can't put his ministry or his job before his family. We need to set our priorities according to God's order. It's not going to make any difference if we work until ten o'clock at night; we still need Jehovah-Jireh to be our Provider. It's not going to make any difference how many people we lay hands on. Nobody getting saved is more important than our families being saved and serving God.

When we do it God's way, our wives will be able to say, "Truly, I have an *'ish*, a man who comes from God." Men, we need to be men of God.

I didn't just get saved thirty-four years ago; I began to serve God. My kids didn't get sent to church; I brought them to church. My kids would see my wife and me praying together. They would see us reading our Bible. They would see us putting our tithes in the offering plate. They would see us lifting up our hands. They would hear us witnessing about Jesus to other people. There's a big difference between an Adam and an *'ish*. There is a big difference between an Eve and an *'ishah*.

Even a Man of God Has "Animal" Needs, Ladies

Here's a big mistake many women make: after they have a baby, all of their energy—physical, emotional, and spiritual—goes toward that child. The animal nature of women says to her husband, "Thank you for housing me, clothing me, and giving me babies, but now, all my energy is going toward the kids." It is natural for a mother's energy to go entirely toward her children, but you aren't natural—you're spiritual. Yes, your children need love, but your husband does, too—and he needs you to show it in a different way.

Males and females have the same basic needs, at least physically speaking. In a spiritual sense, however, their needs vary vastly. The woman doesn't necessarily need a sexual relationship, especially after she's given birth and has children to take care of. But that doesn't mean that her husband's physical needs go away! Even if most of your energy is devoted to changing diapers and cleaning spaghetti off of the wall, you can't afford to forget your husband's needs.

So, by saying, "I have a man from the Lord," Eve was also reminding herself, "I can't afford to be animalistic and devote all of my energy to my baby. I still need to give physical, sexual, and emotional energy to my husband."

Most women want to marry a man they view as their knight in shining armor—an aggressive, manly. They don't want to marry a wimp! But they need to remember that every knight has a libido beneath that armor. In the *Talmud*, it literally teaches that the manlier the man, the stronger is his libido. If you're married to a manly man, you've got to understand his drive. The greater the leader, the greater the drive.

The Man's Sexual Need Is Legitimate

The truth is, most people want to be with someone of the opposite sex, whether from a sense of physical need or emotional longing. If you don't have that need, you're gifted, like the apostle Paul, who affirmed that is not for everyone.

To the church at Corinth, he wrote,

For I wish that all men were even as I myself. But each one has his own gift from God, one in this manner and another in that. But I say to the unmarried and to the widows: It is good for them if they remain even as I am; but if they cannot exercise self-control, let them marry. For it is better to marry than to burn with passion....Are you bound to a wife? Do not seek to be loosed. Are you loosed from a wife? Do not seek a wife....He who is unmarried cares for the things of the Lord; how he may please the Lord. But he who is married cares about the things of the world; how he may please his wife. There is a difference between a wife and a virgin. The unmarried woman cares about the things of the Lord, that she may be holy both in body and in spirit. But she who is married cares about the things of the world; how she may please her husband. (1 Corinthians 7:7–9, 27, 32–34)

But most of us have this need.

However, if you're a wife, you shouldn't expect your husband to talk to you about his needs. The four words men dread the most are these: "We need to talk." We don't even know what that phrase means.

If you aren't tending to your husband's needs, he isn't going to tell you; he'll just get grumpy. If his mood lightens, and you haven't been meeting his sexual needs, he might be getting those needs met in a different way. There's no excuse for extramarital affairs—we aren't animals, and so we have the ability to control our drives. But women need to understand that no number of children will stifle the male's urge for sex. The manlier your husband, the stronger his drive. And the Bible says that you are not to deny those needs.

Let the husband render to his wife the affection due her, and likewise also the wife to her husband. The wife does not have authority over her own body, but the husband does. And likewise the husband does not have authority over his own body, but the wife does. Do not deprive one another except with consent for a time, that you may give yourselves to fasting and prayer; and come together again so that Satan does not tempt you because of your lack of self-control.   (1 Corinthians 7:3–5)

"Fasting" from sex is to be done by mutual consent. Second to "We need to talk," the words husbands most hate to hear are these: "Not tonight, honey; I have a headache." Sex is not dirty. God gave us the drive to engage in it. But the difference is that we aren't animals, and so we don't sleep with someone unless it's our spouse. "Oh, but we're in love!" No, you're not. You're in heat, like the animals. Love is a commitment, and it's a sacrifice of self, especially when you have children. At that point, the man must resist his nature and love those children instead of acting like an animal. At the same time, the woman can't devote all of her energy to her kids—she needs to save some for her man.

Sex Is Not "Dirty"

One source of many Christians' misunderstanding of sex is the church, which has taught that sex is dirty. Sex is not dirty! It's a gift from God. The teaching that says that a man of God must be celibate is complete bunk. Think about it: What was the first commandment God gave to the human race? It wasn't "Don't eat from the tree." The first charge God gave to man and woman was this: *"Be fruitful and multiply"* (Genesis 1:28). How else was mankind to multiply other than by sex?

> *The first charge God gave to man and woman was this: "Be fruitful and multiply" (Genesis 1:28).*

According to Jewish wisdom, if you're a rabbi or a great man of God, you're expected to have a lot of children. Why? Because they want you to pass along your wisdom to your seed. Yet, for so many years, religion has said, "If you're a man of God, abstain from sex." Even now, some religious leaders insist that the sole purpose of sex is procreation, never for simple recreation. But the Bible says, *"Be fruitful and multiply."* To ensure that His command would be fulfilled, God gave the man—the *'ish*—a need for sex. And He put within the *'isha* an interest in her husband and a devotion to her children.

Keep the Flame Alive

It may come as a surprise to know that there is a supernatural way—a hidden biblical mystery—about keeping the heat in your marriage. A key is to remember that we are the temple of God. *"For you are the temple of the living God. As God has said: 'I will dwell in them and walk among them. I will be their God, and they shall be*

My people'" (2 Corinthians 6:16). And so, what was once in the physical temple is now to be seen in the spiritual temple.

But let me describe to you the physical temple. The physical temple described in the Old Testament had an inner court, which represents marriage and the home. Let me explain. There, the two main features were the menorah, which represented the spiritual aspect of life, and the showbread, to symbolize the physical needs of life. Neither worked without the other. To the table, they would bring twelve loaves of showbread every Sabbath. Again, this was to represent all of the family's physical needs—needs pertaining to employment, the home, the family, and even the sexual relationship between two spouses.

The menorah, which represents the spiritual side of life, shows that the light of God has to be lit over the physical aspects of life, or all of our physical efforts will be in vain. Success in our careers, education, marriages, families, and so forth requires that we add our physical to God's spiritual. The two have to work together.

Bread Symbolism in the Bible

Many times, when the Bible talks about eating—specifically, eating bread— it is talking about a sexual experience. Consider the Song of Solomon, which is basically a sex manual for married couples. (Granted, when you read the English translation, you miss a lot.) But in this book about the sexual relationship between a husband and wife, we read, *"Eat, O friends! Drink, yes, drink deeply, O beloved ones!"* (Song of Solomon 5:1). It isn't talking about going out to grab a burger.

Remember when Moses defended Reuel's daughters from a group of shepherds?

> *When they came to Reuel their father, he said, "How is it that you have come so soon today?" And they said, "An Egyptian delivered us from the hand of the shepherds, and he also drew enough water for us and watered the flock." So he said to his daughters, "And where is he? Why is it that you have left the man? Call him, that he may eat bread."*   (Exodus 2:18–20)

Moses did more than eat "bread." *"Then Moses was content to live with the man, and he gave Zipporah his daughter to Moses"* (verse 21). In the Bible, eating— especially bread—often speaks symbolically of the marriage relationship.

A Secret Purpose of the Sabbath

Right after God created man, He created the Sabbath. On the sixth day, *"God created man in His own image"* (Genesis 1:27), and He told him, *"Be fruitful and multiply"* (verse 28). The following day—the seventh day—God *"ended His work which He had done, and He rested on the seventh day from all His work which He had done. Then God blessed the seventh day and sanctified it, because in it He rested from all His work which God had created and made"* (Genesis 2:2–3).

How do we keep the fire of God in our home? The twelve breads represent the reproducing of the children of Israel. They represent reproduction—material, financial, and sexual. And so, on the Sabbath, they would bring in twelve new loaves of bread, which the priest would consume while they were still warm. How did those twelve loaves stay warm for seven days? This is where we get the word "heat" in relation to animals in mating season.

If we do marriage God's way, God will keep the heat and passion in the house, so that it doesn't go out to anybody else. How does that happen? There are no longer twelve showbreads, but God can still keep the heat in our homes, supernaturally, from one Sabbath to another. How? When we do *Shabbat*, we take two loaves, each one with six strands. One loaf represents the blessing of God, while the other loaf represents the relationship between husband and wife. When we put these together, and husband and wife have sex during the week, the Spirit of God pours out on them. Ancient wisdom teaches that if we have sex on the Sabbath, the *shekinah* glory of God is manifested more than at any other time because we are fulfilling *Shabbat* and marrying God's Spirit into their family.

One of the top commandments concerning *Shabbat* is never to be negative. From Friday night to Saturday night, we are forbidden by God to talk about bills, problems, and any unfortunate things that may be going on. Why? Because nothing kills the libido more than arguments about paying the bills, raising the kids, and so forth. This is one reason God commands us to guard the Sabbath and keep it holy! It's a way of supernaturally keeping the fire going in our marriages. We may be too tired on Monday; we may have a soccer game to watch on Tuesday and a business meeting to attend on Wednesday. But, come Friday night, we don't talk about business, soccer, or household problems. On Friday night, we marry God's Spirit to our homes, so that the fire of God will not go out. One man we know brings fresh flowers home every Friday, takes a shower, and dresses in good clothes to show respect and honor to the night and affection to his wife.

The Bible says, *"Marriage is honorable among all, and the bed undefiled"* (Hebrews 13:4). We can't afford to let the world defile the marriage bed! Here's a little marriage counseling 101: if we fight with our spouse at eight o'clock, we shouldn't expect to have sex at ten o'clock. So, God says, "I forbid you to fight. You are My temple. You still have twelve loaves of showbread, and I have a way to keep it warm from Sabbath to Sabbath, no matter how stressful your job is, no matter how many bills you have to pay, no matter how demanding your kids are."

Keeping our "bread" warm is just as spiritual was working a job, being there for our kids, putting food on the table, and worshipping God. Listen: there's going to be a fire! And the greater leadership we have, the greater the fire is! But if we pursue God's way and will, it won't be an out-of-control forest fire but a powerful, raging fire from the throne room of God.

We have this commandment from God: *"And you shall set the showbread on the table before Me always"* (Exodus 25:30). On *Shabbat*, everything comes in twos: we light two candles, we have two angels guarding us and our family, and there are to be two lovers. Amen? (If you're married, that is—not if you're engaged or "in heat.")

Deuteronomy 24:5 offers instructions to a newlywed husband. It says, *"When a man has taken a new wife, he shall not go out to war or be charged with any business; he shall be free at home one year, and bring happiness to his wife whom he has taken."* The Hebrew word for *"happiness"* in this verse literally means "intense sexual pleasure." Now, why would God command the husband to stay home and bring intense sexual pleasure to his wife? Because, when a couple first gets married, the wife is into it just as much as her husband. But then, after a while, her attentions may start to drift toward managing the household and raising her children. And so, the hidden message for ladies is this: one year into a marriage, it may not be as good as it once was. But you still have needs—food, shelter, protection. And your husband has needs, too—at least on *Shabbat*.

Once, when I was studying this subject with some orthodox rabbis, I was a little shocked when they told me that even Jesus knew this. That's why He told the Pharisees who complained about "unlawful" behavior on the Sabbath, *"The Sabbath was made for man, and not man for the Sabbath"* (Mark 2:27). In other words, man was not made to serve the Sabbath through tedious, legalistic tasks. Rather, the Sabbath was created for the benefit of man.

There can be a lot of stress in the home Monday through Friday. We need to get the kids off to school, cook dinner, go to work, do the laundry—I don't think I need to go on. But, come Friday night, let's stop the chaos! Friday night is the time to marry ourselves to the Lord. That's why we have the term "Sabbath bride." We marry it to God. And what God does in the spiritual, He also does in the physical, which is why He said that the Sabbath was made to serve man. On the Sabbath, we stop worrying about the bills, the cooking, and the business deal we're hoping to seal. Listen—if we lose our marriage in the natural, we're at a higher risk of losing our marriage to the Lord, as well.

Marriage confers a responsibility on the man and the woman to act toward each other the way God says to act. Those who get married have a responsibility. When the husband does his part and the wife does hers, the result is a fire of passion by God's design, and not of destruction.

Points to Ponder and Apply

+ Any male can procreate, but that doesn't make him a man.

+ As humans, we have the very breath of God within us; we were created to be different from the animals, and we are not to act like them.

+ Taking responsibility for your decisions is the first step toward change and reward.

+ Provision alone is not enough to keep even the wealthiest of families together. Men, never forget the importance of spending quality time with your families as you train up your children and lovingly support your wife.

+ Not everyone is called to marry; God calls some to be single. Yet even single people have a family—their relatives, as well as their church family.

+ The Sabbath—from Friday to Saturday, sundown to sundown—is a gift to us from God.

Chapter 4

15 HABITS OF HAPPY COUPLES

All marriages are happy. It's the living together
afterward that causes all the trouble.
—Raymond Hull

She said:

One thing that Larry and I have found out as we've ministered to people all over the world, from all nationalities, cultures, and situations, is that everyone is looking for happiness. Each person, no matter his walk of life, is searching for satisfaction and fulfillment. But, for most people, fulfillment alone isn't enough—they want someone special to share it with. So, whether you're currently married, engaged, or hoping to get married someday, this message is for you. God has not called every person to marriage, but marriage is a part of His plan for many people, and He designed it to be a good thing. According to Proverbs 18:22, *"He who finds a wife finds a good thing, and obtains favor from the* Lord." We're going to discover how to make our marriages far better than just "good" with the following habits.

Habit #1: Leave and Cleave

We read in Genesis 2:23–24, *"And Adam said: 'This is now bone of my bones and flesh of my flesh; she shall be called woman, because she was taken out of man.' Therefore a man shall leave his father and mother and be joined to his wife, and they shall become one flesh."* Those are two nice, simple sentences. In real life, however, it takes a whole lot more than two sentences to work out what I like to call the "leavin' and the cleavin'." What does it mean to "leave and cleave"? It means that when we get married, some of our former ties—relationships, friends, hangouts, habits, and all that jazz—need to be let go. It's a universal principle that we need to say no to some things in order to say yes to some other things. In order to say yes to our spouse at the altar—to say yes to a wonderful marriage and a happy home—we need to say no to casual flirting, going out with the boys, and so forth.

It can be a dangerous thing to get married and assume that we can keep on hanging around the same people and doing the same things as before.

I was watching a special on *Oprah* about marriage. The episode was titled "Why Men Cheat." The visiting expert was a man named M. Gary Neuman. He wasn't teaching from a biblical perspective, but he made some excellent points about marriage that Larry and I found absolutely valid.

One thing Mr. Neuman addressed was areas in which couples get into trouble. He talked about the high incidence of divorce—especially serial divorce, with people marrying one person after another and bringing their kids into each new marriage. He said something along the lines of, "We're producing generations and multitudes of messed-up people because we aren't learning how to do marriage right." Then, he said something that startled me: according to his research, 77 percent of the men who cheat on their wives have best friends who also cheated on their wives. Meanwhile, a surveyed group of men who were faithful to their wives said less than 50 percent of their friends cheated in their marriages. What does that reveal to us? In most cases, we become who we hang out with.

Granted, we can't alienate ourselves completely. But we can live in the world and not *live like* the world. We don't have to be affected by those around us. Let's safeguard our hearts with the Word of God—a firewall to stop all worldly influences from infiltrating our lives. We don't have to think about the things our friends are thinking about. We don't need to let our mind drift into areas where it doesn't belong. When we said "I do" and "I will," we also said "I don't" and "I won't." In order to build a strong marriage, there are some unhealthy behaviors we need to leave behind.

Again, I'm not saying that we can't keep our old friends, only that we shouldn't hang on to any friendships that hinder our faithful commitment to our spouse. We're going to get out of marriage what we put into it. Even if our past relationships aren't toxic, per se, spending an overabundance of time with those people may detract from the quality time we should be spending with our spouse.

In our case, for example, Larry likes to golf with his buddies and our sons. I am not a golfer, and I think that it's great that he can get out for some exercise and enjoyment. Meanwhile, I like to go to the mall and shop. Larry hates shopping, and he is happy when I take off with the girls for a day of "fellowshopping." But we are careful not to allow these pastimes to dominate our schedules or to detract from the time we spend together.

Someone might think, *Well, it's not hurting any-body. It's totally benign. You know, I'm not that involved.* But where we put our heart, where we spend our time, is going to grab hold of our heart. The Bible says, *"Where your treasure is, there your heart will be also"* (Matthew 6:21; Luke 12:34 NIV, NKJV). It's the same

> *Where we spend our time is where our hearts will end up.*

principle. Where we spend our time is where our hearts will end up. I always advise people, "Don't go looking outside your marriage for something that's lacking within your marriage."

Habit #2: Build a Foundation of Trust

Trust is elementary in a marriage. I used to say to my kids, "If you lie to me one time, in your mind, you might be thinking, *But I lied just once.* In my mind, I'm thinking, *Was that lie just one of many?* How much more in a marriage! It's often tempting to tell "little white lies" or to cover up things we don't consider too important. Yet it's best to be up-front about everything, no matter how trivial it may seem to us. If we're doing something we don't want our spouse to know about, then we probably shouldn't be doing it.

My husband travels a lot. He's not out there on the road wondering what I'm doing at home. He may be wondering what I'm buying, but he isn't wondering what I'm doing or who I'm with. He trusts me completely because I've proven myself completely trustworthy. Likewise, when Larry's out there on the road, I'm not worried about who he's with or what he's doing. I'm not waking up at two o'clock in the morning thinking, *Oh my gosh! Who is he with?* He is completely trustworthy. We may have had our fair share of arguments in the past, but neither of us has ever wandered in another direction. We have earned one another's trust.

If we have had reason to mistrust our spouse, or if our spouse has had reason to doubt our faithfulness, we need to build the trust back up. We can't be unfaithful one day, the next day say, "I've changed," and expect our spouse to believe us. We have to prove that we've changed over the course of time—days, weeks, even years. It takes a long time to build trust.

I remember reading a story about a woman who had a habit of nagging her husband. One day, she read a book about how to have a great marriage, and she decided, "I'm going to change my ways and become the perfect wife. I'll be so nice to my husband, and everything will change in our marriage." When he came home from work that night, she was dressed in a cute little evening outfit, and she had a candlelit dinner waiting for him on the table. Rather than reacting with the exuberance she had expected, though, he shuffled over to the living room, sat down, and turned on the television. Indignant, the wife said, "Here I am, trying so hard—changing everything—and you don't even notice or appreciate it. Can't you see the effort I'm making?" The husband replied, "Honey, I've seen you try to change about a thousand times. Give me a month or two. If I see that this change lasts, then I'll get excited about it."

When there are issues to deal with, we need to give them time. New habits can take a long time to establish. Someone might say, "Today, I'm going to be different. I'm going to zip my lip. I'm going to be so nice." However, it may take a lot longer than just one day to make that change. Building trust takes more time than almost anything else, especially after it's been broken. But trust is everything, because trust fosters love. It's hard to have love and emotional connection in a relationship that's lacking trust.

Don't be discouraged or overwhelmed. Instead, decide to start fresh. Build toward a consistent positive change, and the desired results will come in due season! The Bible tells us not to grow weary in doing good, for we will reap a reward in due season. (See Galatians 6:9.) Sometimes, a huge miracle comes in the form of hundreds of tiny miracles, so be patient and trust that God is doing a wonderful work in your marriage and family.

Habit #3: Show Some Respect

There is a spirit in the world that says it's cool to treat others as inferior by disrespecting (or "dissing") them with superior attitudes and hurtful, condescending words. Let's get away from the worldly habits of rolling our eyes, sighing, scoffing, and other behaviors that cause our spouses to feel belittled. I see couples treating each other this way all the time.

Whenever Larry or I make this mistake, we have learned to turn it around by quickly apologizing, asking for forgiveness, and moving on. Nobody likes to be made to feel stupid. It's harder for me to get over that feeling than almost any other type of affront. I don't want to be around people who constantly make me feel like I'm ignorant and inferior or that I do everything wrong. I want friends who are going to minimize my faults, focus on my good points, and build me up.

How much more do I want my spouse to do that! The home should be the place where we run for safety and affirmation, not the place we run away from to escape belittling treatment and condescension. Home is to be a place where we're built up, not belittled—a haven of love and acceptance, where we feel the greatest sense of healthy self-confidence. We should feel more confident than ever when we're around our spouses and while we're at home.

I heard a story the other day, though the scenario is by no means uncommon. The husband had fallen into infidelity. (Before I go any further, keep in mind that there is no excuse for infidelity, but there are contributing factors on both sides of the marriage that can help prevent such an outcome, if we'll only learn to recognize them and put them into practice.) Now, this couple had sought counseling. As the husband was telling his side of the story, he explained, "I work hard every day. My wife is a stay-at-home mom. One day, I came home after working twelve hours, and my wife said to me, 'You're not working hard enough to support this family. You need to get a better job where you're making more money for this family.'" He was deeply hurt because he was giving everything he could to support the family, and his wife did not seem grateful for his efforts.

> *We should be our spouse's greatest cheerleader—the wind beneath his or her wings.*

Meanwhile, at work, one of his coworkers had said, "You are just the greatest worker—I wish everyone could see how hard you work. You are worthy of a promotion." And so, what happened? His heart had been hurt at home, while, at work, a coworker had given him the respect and affirmation he'd been desperately seeking. It opened him up as he endeavored to fill his emotional need, and he had an affair with her.

Now, I'm not discussing the affair right now—I'm discussing the events that led up to it. When Larry and I counsel married couples, we try to help the husband and wife to see things from the perspective of their spouse. We always try to treat the source, not just the symptoms. Sometimes, we have to say, "Your spouse may have had an affair, but you kind of played a part in causing it to happen. Can you identify any emotional factors or tangible events that may have set the stage for this? Let's fix the problem so that your spouse doesn't go down that road again."

We should be our spouse's greatest cheerleader—the wind beneath his or her wings. Whether our spouse deserves it or not, let's determine to treat him or her like the king or queen of the castle at the end of the workday. Otherwise, if our spouse spends all day being respected, acknowledged, and appreciated, only to come home to an environment of disrespect, ingratitude, and condescension, chances are, he or she will prefer to be anywhere but at home with us.

On the other hand, our spouse might spend all day being disrespected or beaten down at work or out in the world. Again, we need to make sure that our home is a haven—a place of love, joy, acceptance, and peace—the place we both want to be more than anywhere else!

It takes great effort to show unconditional respect. After all, we tend to let our hair down and show our true colors around the people we spend the most time with. So, we need to be intentional about building up our spouse through words and actions that convey admiration and appreciation. And we need to do it in such a way that we give our spouse something he or she can't get from anyone else.

We are all on a journey of growing and changing. We all have areas that are in need of improvement. In our marriages, let's be sure to "accentuate the positive and eliminate the negative"! Let's also remember the Golden Rule: "Do unto others, including your spouse, as you would have them do unto you." (See, for example, Matthew 7:12.)

Habit #4: Guard Your Heart

The writer of Proverbs says, "*Above all else, guard your heart, for it is the wellspring of life*" (Proverbs 4:23 NIV). We alone have control over the thoughts that our minds entertain. All of our life decisions flow out of our thought lives. That's sobering, but it's also empowering. Here's a helpful illustration: Sow a thought, reap and act; sow a habit, reap a destiny. In short, our thoughts turn into our conversations; our conversations turn into our actions and form our habits; and our habits become our destiny. Every negative thought has negative consequences and repercussions, just as every positive thought has consequences and repercussions. God has entrusted us each with a powerful choice and a powerful force!

When negative thoughts, doubts, and fears come knocking, we have a choice whether to let them in or not. Let's refuse to dwell on them! We may be driving down the highway, thinking about nothing in particular, when, all of a sudden, a negative thought pops into our brain. If we admit it into our mind, we'll start mulling it over, again and again.

We all deal with this in many forms and circumstances of life. Recently, this happened to me. I was driving down the highway by myself when, out of the blue, I began thinking about a negative situation that had happened several years prior. Pretty soon, I was so engrossed in my negative thoughts that I stopped paying attention to the road. Five minutes later, I regained awareness long enough to realize I was traveling at 80 miles an hour, with my hands in a death grip on the steering wheel! I thought, *What are you doing giving so much effort and time to something that happened two years ago? Stop it! Just stop it!* To further convince myself, I reasoned, *What a waste of time. What a waste of brain matter. What a waste of energy. What a waste of emotions. That person ripped me off two years ago, but I'm not going to give that person another ounce of brain matter. It's over. I'm moving on.*

Someone may say, "Fine. I won't speak retaliatory words. But you'd better believe I'll be thinking them." It's like a little boy whose mother told him to go sit in the corner until he got his attitude turned around. After much protesting, he finally went to the corner and sat down, as ordered, but then he said, "I may be sitting on the outside, but I'm standing on the inside."

Sometimes, our outward behavior is right, but it's contradicted by an attitude we're harboring in our hearts. Outward behavior is a good place to start, but let's not stop there. The Lord wants us to have a change of heart, as well as a change of behavior. Life is too short to live with a bad mood all the time. Someone may have ripped us off in the past, but let's not give him one ounce of our future!

Probably every married person has had the unpleasant experience of a morning spat with his or her spouse. If our spouse says something in the morning that irks us, and if we don't let it go, then we'll spend our day kicking ourselves for failing to come up with a clever response—or trying to craft a clever response we'll never use. What terrible bondage! If we fail to take the high road, we'll hold the offense in our heart until we have a chance to get even. I know exactly how this works, because it works this way in me. Human nature is an expert at collecting offenses. We store them up in our memories and turn them over and over in our minds, meticulously crafting an appropriate response or reaction that will put our offender in his or her place. If this tendency describes you—and it describes most of us—arrest those thoughts and take them into captivity! (See 2 Corinthians 10:5.)

Let's follow the instructions of the apostle Paul in Philippians 4:8:

Whatsoever things are true, whatsoever things are honest, whatsoever things are just, whatsoever things are pure, whatsoever things are lovely, whatsoever things are of good report; if there be any virtue, and if there be any praise, think on these things. (KJV)

We must refuse to dwell on the negative. Let's forgive, forget, and move forward. This is crucial in our marriages, as well as in all of our relationships.

Habit #5: Pursue Peace and Unity

Where there is unity, God will command the blessing—including life forevermore! (See Psalm 133:1, 3.) What a powerful promise we have in this Scripture! When we choose harmony and unity over strife and division, God will send a blessing into our marriages and homes.

Sometimes, problems stem from a generational curse that needs to be severed. In other instances, there is simply a learned pattern of behavior that is not conducive to a happy marriage. We can't blame everything on the devil. Much of the time, the root cause of marital discord isn't spiritual; it's the simple, everyday things and irritating habits that corrode a couple's contentment. The Bible says that it's the little foxes that spoil the vine. (See Song of Solomon 2:15.) It's often the little things that add up and ultimately destroy a marriage.

God empowers us to change, true, but He also has given us the ability to make choices. We don't have to model our marriages after those we see in the media or the movies. From a biblical standpoint, most of those aren't acceptable. We may laugh at the spousal spats on such shows as *Everybody Loves Raymond* or *Real Housewives*, but they aren't what God intended for us. Wives are not meant to demean their husbands, and vice versa. When that's our reality, it isn't funny at all. We need to spend time and effort creating a home atmosphere that's full of love, acceptance, and joy.

There are two slogans I often see on bumper stickers and T-shirts—"If Momma ain't happy, ain't nobody happy" and "Caution: Explosive Temper!" These sayings may strike some people as humorous, but to those who live in a household where these slogans are the norm, there is nothing funny about them at all. There's nothing worse than feeling as if you have to walk on eggshells in your own home.

A friend of mine told me that when she was a kid, she could always tell when her mother was paying the bills. She'd know it the moment she walked in the door after school. Even before she saw her mother, she could sense a tangible heaviness when her mother was paying the bills. And some people are proud of having that type of power in their homes! Unfortunately, many people use emotional blackmail to control and manipulate their spouses and other family members. These families are ticking time bombs. If we are going to see the blessings of God in our homes, we have to do some emotional housekeeping. Let me assure you that as soon as we begin to move forward, God is right there to help us!

The Bible instructs us, *"Do not let the sun go down on your wrath, nor give place to the devil"* (Ephesians 4:26–27). What useful guidance! The most important times of the day are the beginning and end—the morning and evening—because it is at those times that we set a mood that will determine the course of our day. Larry has a teaching on *modeh ani*, which is the Hebrew term used to describe what we should pray each and every morning: "Thank You, Lord, for waking me and giving me life. Thank You for restoring my soul with compassion and for breathing Your breath of life into me."[1] Beginning each morning with an attitude of gratitude and a spirit of joy sets a positive course for the entire day. Even on the busiest of mornings, let's choose joy and avoid negativity.

In the same way, at the end of the day, avoid spats and arguments at all costs. There is nothing worse than trying to sleep after an argument: you toss and turn all night, thinking it over, and the problem is still there for you to deal with when you wake up in the morning. If an issue arises, do everything within your power to resolve it before you go to sleep at night. Realize that there is much more at stake than just winning this argument. Take the high road. Be the peacemaker. Initiate peace. Ask forgiveness and forgive your spouse. Pull every ugly thought into captivity. Choose to focus on the positive. If you have to discuss a challenge or a problem, be sure to end the conversation on a note of hope by affirming your faith in God's promises.

Every time we make a choice to bring peace into our home, every time we assume the role of peacemaker; every time we choose to give up something for the

---

[1]For Larry's teaching on *modeh ani*, refer to Larry Huch, *Unveiling Ancient Biblical Secrets* (New Kensington, PA: Whitaker House, 2011), 159–174.

When we consistently choose to act and speak in ways that will move us closer to our spouse, we progress along the path toward becoming one.

sake of a loved one; every time we rein in our negative thoughts and put a guard on our mouth; every time we forgo retaliation; every time we forgive willingly—every time we make even the simplest of choices that will benefit our family—God sees, and He says, "I'm going to command a blessing on you and your house." It isn't just a single choice on our wedding day—"Well, I'm choosing to get married, and now we'll live happily ever after." That's only the beginning of a lifetime of choices, from major decisions to small, everyday judgment calls. When we consistently choose to act and speak in ways that will move us closer to our spouse, we progress along the path toward becoming one.

Habit #6: Take the High Road

In our early years of marriage, Larry and I had a lot of growing to do. We had a lot of what I call "intense fellowship." It seemed like we were continually coming up against the same brick wall. He was dealing with an anger problem; I was dealing with contentiousness, unforgiveness, and all kinds of negative emotions. Whenever an emotional spark ignited, we would take turns pouring kerosene on top to create quite a firestorm! Finally, we came to a point where we both felt so miserable and guilty that we said to each other, "We've got to stop this. Let's get our act together. We're going to change—grow up and start acting like mature Christian adults. Let's break this negative, downward cycle!"

One day not long after that, we were driving along, and an issue came up. I can't remember what it was. All of a sudden, one of us started—"Blah, blah, blah"—and the other replied, "Blah blah blah," and on and on. After a little bit, I thought, *I'm not going to say anything back.* So, I simply remained silent. Well, to be honest, "simply" isn't accurate, because I really wanted to retaliate verbally. I gave myself an internal pep talk: *You know what? I'm not going to fight. I'm not going there. Let's just calm down; take things down a notch or two; smile and be happy.* After that, I just looked over and smiled at Larry, and then I reached over, hugged him, and gave him a big smack (a kiss, not a violent slap) on the cheek. I said, "I really don't want to argue with you. I love you too much to fight with you." With my words, I defused the situation. Larry said that he didn't want to fight with me, either, and, just like that, it was over. I thought, *Wow! That was pretty easy. I really learned something here today.* I was so proud of myself. That's why I remember it to this day. That was thirty-five years ago. Let's not make it so difficult. It's easy! We just need to choose to stop.

I guarantee that all of us will have disagreements. Conflict is a part of human nature. Learning to resolve conflicts in a peaceful, godly way is a tremendous attribute and asset in every area of our lives. So, learn to be the peacemaker! Take the high road! Be the one who breaks the downward cycle! Cover each other, and cut each other some slack!

> *Learning to resolve conflicts in a peaceful, godly way is a tremendous attribute and asset in every area of our lives.*

Occasionally, I can get a little irritable, and Larry will take the high road and arrest the situation. Other times, Larry is the one on edge. I will take the high road and head off what otherwise could have become a contentious argument. We each have to step up and extend forgiveness instead of retaliating with a similar attitude and "getting back" at each other.

Each of us is a work in progress, so let's cut our spouses some slack. Maybe your husband snaps at you, on occasion; maybe your wife rolls her eyes. Let's not turn it into World War III. Let's take the high road of maturity, get over it, and move forward. We shouldn't let one attitude-tinged reaction ruin our day or our week. It isn't worth it. There's too much blessing at stake!

There's a new term being used in our generation, and it's pretty pathetic: "kidults." Each of us probably knows someone for whom this term is fitting—a kid who has grown into adulthood but still acts like a kid. Apparently, this trend is so widespread in our society that it needed to be given a name.

The other day, while I was getting my nails done at the salon, I saw these two little girls, probably sisters, start to spar with each other. One of them said, "You're a tattletale," and the other responded, "*You're* a tattletale." Her sister protested, "No, you tattled on me." "No, *you* tattled on *me!*" "No, *you* did!" Back and forth they went. Before you knew it, they were bawling and screaming. Typical behavior for three- and five-year-olds, maybe, but it shouldn't be typical for adults! Life is too short for such petty fighting.

We know how to push one another's buttons, don't we? When our kids were young, our son, Luke, sure liked provoking his sisters. He knew exactly what to do to set them off. He knew their hot spots. I would tell Anna and Katie, "Don't give him the satisfaction of a response. He'll stop if he can't get you riled up." If a little boy is pulling on the pigtails of a little girl, all he wants is to hear her squeal.

We see this same chain reaction between married adults, except with much more at stake. We can't afford to play along! Walking away is often the best thing to do to defuse the situation. If we react, we're only rewarding the provoker with the satisfaction he or she seeking. We know exactly what sets off our spouse. Let's refuse to be kidults and choose maturity, instead. As we mature spiritually, let's also grow in the natural.

I've heard it said, "Problems not dealt with don't go away; they go underground only to resurface later." There are issues that arise in marriage that need to be discussed and resolved. However, we often hear worldly "wisdom" directing us, saying, "Speak your mind. Don't hold in what you're feeling. Be true to yourself. Be honest. Tell people exactly what you think of them." Oftentimes, this is a recipe for failed relationships. The Bible says that we are to put every negative thought into captivity and speak only words of kindness. (See 2 Corinthians 10:5.) And the apostle James instructs us, "*So then, my beloved brethren, let every man be swift to hear, slow to speak, slow to wrath; for the wrath of man does not produce the righteousness of God*" (James 1:19–20). For the most part, only good should come out of our lips.

Let's put a little zip on our lip that keeps anything negative from escaping. When we're tempted to say something negative, we just zip it. We hold it back. We avoid speaking those negative things. You know the saying, "Sticks and stones will break my bones, but words can never hurt me"? That's one of the biggest lies that's ever been told. If we think back to childhood, we probably don't remember falling down and skinning our knee at the age of eight, but we do remember the hurtful things that were said to us then.

Hurtful, malicious comments weasel their way into our hearts and rarely go away. How much more so in a marriage? When we say hurtful things in a marriage, there's no getting away from it. When we're kids, and we say hurtful things to a friend, he may not be our friend next year. And, while friends may come and go—we may not mind losing one—a spouse is supposed to be forever. Marriage is for life. If someone wants to speak his mind, voice his opinion, and clear the air, he needs to know that he will pay a hefty price for it. Those hurtful words will take root in the heart of his spouse, and it will take a long time for the pain to wear off. So, let's be sure to weigh our words and count the cost of what we're saying.

Let's learn to say to ourselves, "I'm taking the high road. I'm over that. I'm bigger than that offense." Every household will have differences of opinion. When conflicts arise, we can resolve them without all of the screaming and yelling and ranting and raving. With God's help, we can work through our issues as mature adults.

Proverbs 14:1 says, "*The wise woman builds her house, but the foolish pulls it down with her hands.*" That applies to men, as well. If we choose wisdom, we'll make wise choices and build a good marriage, raise good children, and establish our houses through the steps God has shown us. Any foolish person can tear something down, no sweat. Think about how little children play. A young boy spends all day building a castle out of Legos, and then along comes a playmate who gives it a kick and, in two seconds, it has toppled. But it takes wisdom, effort, and diligence to build something—especially something worth keeping. When we take the high road, we act as builders rather than those who tear down.

> *It takes wisdom, effort, and diligence to build something—especially something worth keeping. When we take the high road, we act as builders rather than those who tear down.*

Many of the major issues we face in life start out as small, manageable flames but go ignored and then grow into raging infernos. If a little fire starts, we can either put it out immediately with some water, or we can let it burn unattended until it's raging out of control. At that point, impulsive actions may only act as fuel to the flames. Let's put out the fires in our marriages as quickly as possible, while they're still small. That way, we'll have a greater chance of staying the course through whatever storms the enemy sends our way, and we will position ourselves to receive a full portion of the blessings of God.

Habit #7: Forgive and Forget

We need to make forgiveness our only option. The Bible says, "*Do not let the sun go down on your wrath*" (Ephesians 4:26). If we have a spat with our spouse, we shouldn't go to sleep until we've cleared the air and made up. The Lord knows all too well how we humans function. He tells us how to start and end our days. Once we master that, everything in between should fall into place!

We're all human, so we'll do things for which we need to be forgiven. It's crucial not to let the sun go down on our wrath. When nighttime rolls around, let's give ourselves a checkup from the neck-up and see if there are any issues that need to be straightened out before we turn out the light. Let's be willing to say we're sorry and to ask for forgiveness, even if we don't believe we were wrong. Let's ask ourselves if we would rather be right or be happy. Being "right" is no fun if you're miserable. Let's choose to take the high road and extend forgiveness, if not for anybody else's sake, then because God says to. We want to go to bed right with God.

Forgiveness is an incredibly powerful force. When we ask to be forgiven, it unleashes the blessings of God in our own hearts. When we choose to forgive someone else, it unleashes an even greater outpouring of blessings into our hearts, because forgiving someone who has wronged us not only frees that person—it frees us, as well. We need to decide to get better, not get bitter!

Bitterness and unforgiveness are toxic attitudes that bind us up from the inside out. Not only do they wreak havoc on our emotional well-being, but they also take a heavy toll on our physical health. Doctors all over the world agree that negative emotions such as anger, hatred, bitterness, unforgiveness, vengeance, worry, fear, and stress play a major role in many diseases. For many years, we have all heard that stress can be a major contributor to heart attacks and heart disease. But new studies are proving that stress and other negative emotions create toxic conditions in our bodies that can contribute to serious illnesses of all kinds. This is sobering information! If not for our spiritual health, then for our physical health, let's keep our hearts and minds free of toxic emotions stemming from resentment and unforgiveness.

Of course, the main reason we need to practice forgiveness is because God tells us to. When Jesus taught His disciples the Lord's Prayer as a template to follow, He established the necessity of asking God for forgiveness *on a daily basis.* We are to pray, "Father, forgive us our sins, just as we forgive those who have sinned against us." (See Matthew 6:12; Luke 11:4.) The Bible says that our own forgiveness and freedom in Christ depends on the degree to which we extend forgiveness and freedom to others. (See Matthew 6:14–15.) Forgiveness begins with a choice, and it becomes a reality through God's grace, help, and equipping.

Choose to forgive. Choose to live free from bitterness, unforgiveness, and other toxic emotions. As you walk in forgiveness, you will mature, becoming more Christlike, not to mention more content. When you sow forgiveness and grace, the harvest you reap will reflect those same blessings. And the more you practice this, the more natural it will become! You will unleash the wonderful blessings of God into your marriage, your family, and all of your relationships. What a great way to live!

Habit #8: Lighten Up

Over the last thirty-five years, Larry and I have had to work hard to achieve a balance between our marriage, our family, and our full-time work in ministry. For us, it's natural to put the ministry first, as we've discussed, and to carry a sense of weight and concern for the state of the world. We can get to a point, however, that we feel a heavy burden for souls, a burden for the lost, a burden for the sins in the world, and a burden for just about everything in heaven and on earth! We can end up so weighted down with all these spiritual burdens that we feel guilty for engaging in any activity that's solely for our personal enjoyment. It can become a troublesome, weighty feeling, and, if left unchecked, it takes a toll on our marriages and families.

This is exactly what started happening to us. Finally, we had to step back and say to ourselves, "Look. We can't carry the burden of the world. We're only human. We can do only so much." We learned how to lighten up. We have always taken our ministry seriously, but there comes a time when we need to disconnect from the heavy burden of our calling, whether we're in ministry, business, or another professional realm. When we get home in the evening, let's leave it at the door. Better yet, let's leave it at the office! When we come home, we need to switch hats.

When we're driving home, it isn't uncommon to rehearse in our mind everything we did that day. Let's just remember to shift gears when we get home. Going into "family mode" prepares us to tackle our job at home—caring for our spouse and children—and to take it as seriously as we do our office job.

A friend of mine who has a very demanding job with many people reporting to her says she has to remind herself of her role as wife when she comes home. When she pulls into her garage after a day at work, she pretends there is a sign on the back wall that reads, "And now you are his wife." This practice helps her to shift her focus and ultimately enables her to contribute to a sense of sweet harmony in her home.

While neither Larry nor I have a sign such as this woman, we are constantly committed to making our home a haven of joy—a place where we prioritize family time and relaxation. Maintaining this mind-set ensures that we refuel ourselves at home so that we're able to meet the demands of full-time ministry.

Habit #9: Choose Joy

I say this all the time: "We're as happy today as we decide to be." Because of human nature, it's our tendency to compare ourselves to others and think, *If only my life was like so-and-so's. If only my husband was like this. If only my wife was like that. If only, if only, if only.* We need to get to the point where we decide to be happy today, regardless of our circumstances.

As an example, let's consider the apostle Paul, who rejoiced even in suffering:

I now rejoice in my sufferings for you, and fill up in my flesh what is lacking in the afflictions of Christ, for the sake of His body, which is the church.

(Colossians 1:24)

Rejoice in the Lord always. Again I will say, rejoice!   (Philippians 4:4)

Rejoice always.   (1 Thessalonians 5:16)

I once heard Dr. James Dobson tell the following story. Someone came up to his wife and said, "Your husband teaches so wonderfully on marriage. He really understands women and how they function. You've got to be the happiest woman in the world." His wife replied, "Dear, he tries very hard to make me happy, but, every day, I have to choose to make myself happy because nobody can come and make us happy."

> *Let's consider ourselves first and see if any change is necessary before we command our spouse to change.*

Every relationship takes two people. In marriage, if the wife is discontent, she ought to look at herself, as well as her husband, to see about remedying the situation. The only person over whom we have complete control is ourselves. Let's consider ourselves first and see if any change is necessary before we command our spouse to change.

Whether we have the "perfect" life or the worst life, we can decide, "It's a good day. This is the day that the Lord has made, so I will rejoice and be glad in it." (See Psalm 118:24.) If somebody asks us, "How are you doing today?" we can say, "I'm doing great. You know why? Because I serve a great God, and I plan to be happy every single day." When we get up in the morning, let's make a choice to be happy. By focusing our thoughts and our spirit on the promises of God and the hope that we have in Him, we can color the way we see everything else in our lives. Accentuate the positive; eliminate the negative.

There have been studies that aimed to find out the secrets of the world's happiest people. It's easy to say, "They're just naturally happy. They have sunny dispositions." In some cases, this is true. For the most part, however, happy people have made a choice. They've programmed themselves to be happy. And that includes the happiness they experience in marriage.

Every marriage has its ups and downs, its strengths and weaknesses. When I married Larry, he was the man of my dreams. I was especially drawn to him because of his identity as a leader—someone assertive who liked to take charge and make things happen. Assertiveness and aggressiveness are good traits! But there are two sides to that coin: the same traits of assertiveness and aggression that I love about him are the traits that can be a particular challenge if we don't see eye to eye on an issue. That's the challenging side of the coin.

The same illustration can be applied to my qualities and how Larry views them. I know that he appreciates my own assertiveness, for the most part; on the flip side, this character trait may not be appreciated quite as much in times of "heated fellowship"!

In each of us, every positive trait has a flip side—the inherent potential to manifest negatively, in certain circumstances. I know people whose positive traits are nearly the opposite of Larry's and mine. For example, we know a couple in which the husband is the most easygoing, levelheaded man we've ever met. It was these traits that attracted his wife to him in the first place, and yet, recently, she came to me and expressed frustration with her husband's lack of drive and motivation. I told her that the traits that were causing her frustration were simply one side of the same coin—they related to his kindhearted, easygoing nature. When we look at our spouse and see only weaknesses and flaws, we're focusing on the negative. We need to focus on the good and work with the bad. Accentuate the positive, and lighten up the negative!

One day, when Larry and I were living in Australia, God spoke to us while we were walking on the beach at sunset. Larry picked up a pebble and studied it. He held it up to his eye, so close that it entirely obscured the setting sun. Think about that—a miniscule pebble blocked out the entire sun! We have the same choice in marriage. We can have a wonderful life, but if we pick up the little, petty rock—perhaps our annoyance with a spouse who doesn't put his or her dirty clothes in the hamper—we magnify the negative aspect, holding it so close until it's all that we see. Let's not block out all of the positive with one tiny negative! Step back and see the good.

It's commonly held that the average human being has about 60,000 thoughts each day—that equates to about one thought per second—and that, of these thoughts, 80 percent are negative. One study I read addressed this issue and said that humans have what is called a "negativity bias," or an inborn tendency to register negative thoughts, feelings, and experiences more acutely than positive ones. For example, after a church service, if ten people tell me they loved the sermon but one person says, "You hurt my feelings," that's the comment that's going to stick with me. If ten people say, "You look great today," but one person comes up to me and says, "Pink and black? Really?" that's what I'll take home with me. We're hardwired to have our feelings hurt due to negative comments that overshadow positive ones. It's natural to register negativity more than we do positivity.

One time, I was teaching before an audience, and I noticed a woman seated in the back with a sour look on her face for the duration of my message. I was certain I was crashing and burning because her scowl never vanished. My entire perception about how my teaching was being received was based on what I believed her emotions to be, as indicated by her facial expression. At the end of my presentation, I saw her make a beeline for me. As she was coming straight at me, I was thinking, *Oh, no. She's going to tell me everything I said wrong and all of the Scriptures I quoted incorrectly.*

Sure enough, she reached me—with tears streaming down her face. She said, "I was so moved by what you said—I was just riveted—and my life has been changed." Boy, had I read that one wrong! If she hadn't come to tell me how she'd received my message, the entire event would have been filed away in my mind as a failure, and my self-esteem would have fallen. One single sour-looking expression had kept me from noticing all of the smiles and looks of appreciation from the rest of the audience!

So, in marriage, as well as in life, we shouldn't be quick to judge others' feelings, because we're prone to misinterpret signs, especially when we're guided by our emotions. It may be tempting to assume that if our spouse isn't saying anything, he or she is annoyed or angry with us. Yet he or she may simply be relaxing. Let's avoid jumping to conclusions!

Sometimes, Larry is sitting there with a look on his face, and I think, *Uh-oh. He's upset about something. What did I do wrong?* only to find out that he's been thinking about his message for the following Sunday. He's focusing,

> *In marriage, as well as in life, we shouldn't be quick to judge others' feelings, because we're prone to misinterpret signs, especially when we're guided by our emotions.*

and I assume he's fuming. Let's not be so quick to assume the worst. Instead, let's stay on the sunny side of life! If we keep our face to the sun, we won't see the shadows. If we're happy today, it's because we decided to be. Sometimes, we smile because we're happy. More often, we're happy because we smiled. And that is absolutely true in marriage. The key is not to get bitter but to get better!

It's crucial to keep a sense of humor—to laugh with each other and to roll with the punches. It also helps to find out what makes our spouse laugh, because laughter is really important. A sense of humor is crucial because it enables us to roll with the punches and laugh it off whenever a situation comes our way. Laughter enhances our ability to enjoy life together.

Habit #10: Be Intentional About Spending Time Together

We have only so much time in a given day to put toward social activity of any kind. If we're at work all day, we're left with only the evenings to build our marriage relationship by spending time with our spouse.

I've heard it said that the average married couple engages in true conversation for only twelve minutes a day. Unbelievable, isn't it? Think about it: so often, we come home from work, and we're together, but we aren't really communicating, other than at a superficial level. We aren't discussing anything of substance. When was the last time you sat down for a one-on-one conversation about deeper things? When was the last time you asked your spouse, "How was your day?" "What projects are you working on at the office?"

Many of us are so tired by the time we get home from work, we don't want to talk to anybody. We just want to sit and veg out in front of the TV. That's okay, to a certain degree, but we never build relationships accidentally. Relationships are built through significant investments of time, interest, and energy, so we need to make big deposits where it counts. Let's not be guilty of giving our best to the world and leaving only leftovers for our families.

Habit #11: Have Fun

I've said that Larry and I became Christians and were launched into ministry in a fellowship that put family at the bottom of the list. Ministry was first; family came last. When we launched our first church, I remember handing out ten thousand flyers for our opening event. Guess whose home phone number was on each of those ten thousand flyers? Ours. We were taught that no sacrifice was too great for the kingdom of God.

We were essentially taught to give our best to everybody else at the expense if our own family. We were expected to sacrifice our home, our children—everything—for the sake of the ministry. After fifteen years, we reached the point of having nothing left to give. That was neither biblical nor wise. See, if the enemy can't get us to slow down for God, he'll get us to speed up for God, to the point where we have no time for our family. What happens then? We can end up getting burned out and even losing our family.

Finally, we noticed some other ministers who were happy, and we followed their example by spending time together and having fun as a family. We already knew how to work together, collaborate on projects, and get the job done. But we didn't know how to have fun together. About that time, a friend of ours from Portland said, "You guys have been working so hard, I want to send you to Hawaii. You can use my air miles and stay in my condo. It will cost you nothing." Generous, right? Guess how Larry and I reacted: "Why would we go to Hawaii? What would we do there? We'd be bored." We really didn't know how to have fun! Now, once our friend forced us to go, we caught the "fun" fever. We figured it out. And we've been vacationing in her condo ever since, because that's where we like to go to regroup, refresh, and replenish our relationship, so that we have something to give to the people we minister to.

Having fun together is incredibly important. Laughter and rejoicing are key ingredients in any successful marriage. They help us to fall in love again, day after day, and they ensure that our relationship does not become businesslike, with a primary focus on keeping up with the housework and paying the bills.

Try adopting the following rules to keep the fun in your relationship:

1. Schedule a weekly or monthly date night, depending on your budget and calendar.

2. When you go out on a date night, don't talk about business, bills, or other burdens.

3. Enjoy each other!

Habit #12: Turn Up the Romance

Almost every married couple is searching for a way to keep their love life alive and thriving. In marriage, a husband and wife share something very special and sacred—something that's exclusive, not to be shared with anyone else. If it's going to stay exclusive, we need to keep romance in the mix. And we've got to work at it. If we take care of business at home, our spouse has no need to roam. So, let's make a habit of scheduling date nights, as I just suggested, and make them special.

Habit #13: Pray Together

A husband and wife should be a spiritual team—a force of faith the enemy can't mess with. When the devil comes against us, we stand up to him together and walk out our faith. We need to make sure that we aren't people of faith only when we're in church or around other Christians. Faith should lead the way in our homes, as well.

Sometimes, I meet with couples, and one spouse is a powerhouse for the Lord, while the other is just a passenger. I tell them, "You've got to be in this together. You've got to be a team." I tell them what the Bible says about being unequally yoked. (See 2 Corinthians 6:14.) Couples who are unequally yoked pull against each other instead of in the same direction, wasting their energy and going nowhere.

Being "unequally yoked" doesn't just mean being married to an unbeliever. It can also mean rushing ahead of your spouse, spiritually speaking, or allowing your spouse to "hitch a ride" on your relationship with God instead of building his or her own relationship with our heavenly Father.

When a couple is serving God together, they present a united front; come hell or high water, whatever the world is doing, they're serving God. It is God's plan to raise up the husband as a man of God who will lead his family rather than be a mere spectator in spiritual things. It's His plan to raise up the wife as a woman similar to the one described in Proverbs 31—a wife who supports her husband, a mother who guides and nurtures her children. The husband and wife, leading side by side.

When a problem hits Larry and me, we immediately speak out the Word. We live by Romans 8:28: *"All things work together for good to those who love God, to those who are the called according to His purpose."* If a problem comes our way, we'll talk about it. We'll dissect it. We'll see how we can make it better or change it. But that conversation is always framed by the assurance that God will work everything together for our good and cause us to emerge victorious. We're not going under; we're going over. Together, as a team, we can calm the spirit in our home as we put the enemy in his place and put God in His place.

If we take a financial hit—and there have been seasons when we have—we say, "That's okay; the devil just owes us seven times the amount he stole from us." (See Proverbs 6:30–31.) Our God is a restorer, and He multiplies back to us everything the enemy has taken. When the economy bottomed out, and everyone was worried, Larry and I got into the Word of God and declared, "Despite everything that's going on to make us doubt our financial solvency, our God is a supplier. He is our supply and our source. We are children of God, and so, though we live in this world, we're not of this world." That was how we stayed the course in the midst of economic turmoil.

The enemy is powerless to do anything unless we let him. That's why we need to be a team who stands in faith against the devil and his wiles. When tests and trials come on the scene, we don't turn our backs on God. Instead, we turn to each other and say, "That's okay, because we're not going under; we're going over." Christian couples need to come together and speak the Word of God over their lives and marriages.

We live in a stormy world. The storms of life will come to all of us at different times. Now, I'm not confessing something negative. I'm just being realistic: that's life. But the storms affect us only if we let them get on the inside of us. There is an old saying: "A little tiny ship can stay afloat on all the oceans of the world if it doesn't let the water get inside." So, when all the world is in chaos, we can stay calm. We can speak to the storm and calm our own spirit, through the power of God. We can stay the course.

One practice we recommend is assembling as a family every Friday night to observe *Shabbat* together. During *Shabbat*, we prophesy over our children, declaring that our daughters will be Proverbs 31 women and our sons will be men of God who walk with integrity and honor. Wives prophesy that their husbands will be spiritual leaders and men of God, full of integrity and righteousness, and that blessings are going to be poured into their families because of their faith. Instead of focusing on all of the things our family has done to frustrate us in the past week, we prophesy all of the things they are going to do right. We envision it and believe it.

> *When all the world is in chaos, we can stay calm. We can speak to the storm and calm our own spirit, through the power of God.*

Remember, God watches over His Word to perform it. (See Jeremiah 1:12 NASB.) When we speak over our family and say, for example, "I will be a Proverbs 31 woman," the promises in His Word will come to pass. Just as God's promise to Abram and Sarai was fulfilled, the promise will become reality. Suddenly, Sarai went from being a cantankerous, contentious woman to Sarah, the princess. God told her, "This is who you're going to be, and I'm going to change your name to prove it." When Abraham and Sarah believed Him, they began to step out of who they had been in the world and to step into what God had for them. Abram became Abraham, the father of many nations. He and Sarah were childless—beyond childbearing age, in fact. But they began to call each other by the names that represented what God had promised them, and then it came to pass: Sarah conceived and gave birth to Isaac.

Habit #14: Make a Plan and Work It

The Bible says, *"Where there is no vision, the people perish"* (Proverbs 29:18 KJV). Even in marriage, we have to make a plan. If we want a better marriage, then we need to draw up some plans to make improvements. And our plans should be based on the ultimate marriage manual: the Word of God.

When we wake up in the morning, let's say to ourselves, "No matter what comes my way today, I'm following this plan. No matter what tries to steal my victory today, I'm following my plan. No matter what gets in my way or what obstacles come into our marriage, we're sticking with this plan. We're going for it."

Habit #15: Give It to God

Maybe you're in a place similar to where we were thirty-five years ago, and you're saying, "God, how can this ever change?" Larry and I went through some really tough times, and that's why we're passionate about building a bridge for you—so that you don't have to experience those tough times. I remember taking a long walk to the top of a hill, where I sat down and cried, sobbing, "God, how is this ever going to change?" We had just had a major fight over some stupid, ridiculous argument, as always. It was horrifying. I said, "God, how can a person ever change in the natural? How can this ever be different?"

But I knew the promises of God, and I grabbed hold of them. I knew that God was bigger than any problem we could ever face and that He would vindicate His Word. I remember sitting there, making the choice to believe, and making the choice to change. I remember praying, "Lord, I can't change him, but You can. And I can change myself. So, I'm not going to worry about him; I'm going to leave him to You. I'm going to do what I need to do in order to make this a better marriage, and I'm going to do what I need to do to become the best spouse he could have."

God can break every curse and reverse every pattern of destruction in our lives.

I distinctly remember doing that. What I don't remember is what we'd been fighting about, because I made a choice to move on. To put it in the past. To learn from it and go forward. I like to say, "I distinctly remember forgetting that." Is that a choice we have to make just one time? Absolutely not! It's a choice we have to make every day, sometimes multiple times a day, especially in marriage. But God, in His goodness and mercy, empowers us to change, regardless of what we're facing now or what we've faced in the past. He can break every curse and reverse every pattern of destruction in our lives.

When we turn everything over to God, we can have the marriage we've always dreamed of—a wonderful friendship and an amazing love affair that gets better and better every year. Let's choose this day—and every day—to be the best we can be for God and for our spouse.

If you're not married, then God is your spouse right now. (See Isaiah 54:5.) And He is carving out the man or woman of your dreams. While you're praying and getting yourself ready, God's getting him or her ready for you. If you have been through a divorce, then God has a new beginning for you. This message is just as much for single people and divorced people as it is for married people because we need to learn how to do it right. We need to learn how to have godly homes, godly marriages, and godly children.

Larry and I have the greatest marriage relationship imaginable. We are best friends, soul mates, teammates, and lovers, and our family is our most precious treasure. Be encouraged: what the Lord has done for us, He wants to do for you, too! Our prayer is that your every dream comes true and that you will experience the reality that God *"is able to do exceedingly abundantly above all that we ask or think, according to the power that works in us"* (Ephesians 3:20). It's time to dream again—to open your heart to receive a new dimension of God's love and blessings. It's time for your new beginning!

Points to Ponder and Apply

+ While marriage is meant to bring joy to our lives, it was never meant to be our ultimate source of happiness and fulfillment.

+ God has placed within each of us a desire for love and acceptance, and He alone—not our soul mate—is truly able to satisfy that desire.

+ A lie is a lie, little and white or not. Be sure to speak the truth in love (see Ephesians 4:15) so that you may build your marriage on a foundation of trust.

+ Be quick to apologize and to extend forgiveness. Avoid rehearsing in your mind what you should have said.

+ Remember that not all issues are demonic; sometimes, problems simply stem from poor choices or bad habits.

+ If there is a generational curse operating in your marriage, break it off, in Jesus' name!

+ Choose joy. You are as happy today as you decide to be. Instead of expecting others to make you happy, look for ways to bring laughter and love to their lives.

+ Change yourself first, and your family will follow.

Chapter 5

SAFEGUARDING YOUR MARRIAGE

*A successful marriage requires falling in love many
times, always with the same person.*
—Mignon McLaughlin

She said:

We live in a world that is very cynical about marriage. A front-page article from *USA Today* entitled "We're just not that into marriage" reported on a study by the Pew Research Center, the results of which indicated a "declining interest" in marriage among Americans. Thirty-nine percent of respondents said that the institution of marriage is "becoming obsolete."[2] We see some celebrities shrug off the fact that they've gotten divorced and remarried as many as eight times! And the divorce rate among professing Christians is as high as the rate among nonbelievers. Obviously, we're missing something, because there are promises of blessings from God that aren't translating into the lives of His children.

Marriage is meant to be more than just passing the time with someone until we get bored with that person and move on to somebody else. Marriage is based on a holy vow that we make before God. It's is a sacred union of two lives brought together by God to become one, and it isn't something to enter into lightly or casually. Of course, there will be obstacles along the way, even for the happiest of married couples. But we are not to abandon ship at the first sign of trouble. We don't throw away our wedding vows because we believe we've reached a point of "irreconcilable differences." With God, all things are possible. (See Matthew 19:26; Mark 10:27; Luke 18:27.) And, if we let Him, He will use the trials and tests of marriage to mold us as individuals, to shape us as a couple, and to strengthen our bond.

Is it really possible for a man and a woman to fall in love, get married, and stay in love? Absolutely. Will there be challenges along the way? Yes, of course. But they are surmountable when we determine not to give up. Believe it or not,

---

[2]Sharon Jayson, "We're just not that into marriage," *USA Today*, 18 November 2010.
http://www.usatoday.com/printedition/news/20101118/1amarriage18_st.art.htm.

a marriage takes a lot of work. There is a tendency among Christians is to say, "We're saved, and we have faith, so we'll just trust God to get us through this." Meanwhile, they're trusting God to do everything, including the work that they themselves need to do! God is a God of restoration, but we need to do what we can to avert divorce and other tragedies.

A Word on Divorce

Before I go any further, let me emphasize that divorce is not an unpardonable sin. Maybe you have been in a difficult relationship or have gotten a divorce. Be encouraged by this note I received via e-mail from a young woman in our church.

> I'm a Christian, and I've raised my kids in the church. Two years ago, my husband and I ended up getting divorced. I thought God was done with me. Every church teaching that I had seen seemed to indicate as much. I'd been taught that, if you got a divorce, you were either going to hell, or you would have to stay single for the rest of your life. But then, I came across a Web site, Lighthouse.com, with one of your teachings. I had never heard of you before. The title of the teaching was "Divorce: Does That Make Me a Second-Class Citizen?" And it was the only teaching I could find that didn't condemn me for being a divorced woman. My life changed drastically because, first of all, I realized that God didn't hate me—I wasn't going to hell—and that He would restore my life. I'm still single, not having found anybody new, but I'm happy and still raising my kids in church. I have confidence that God is in my corner, paving out a path of destiny for my life.

Amen! I couldn't have said it better myself. God is never pointing a finger of accusation at us; He's always reaching out a hand to help us. He fixes our messes. And what we're discussing now is how to avoid making any more messes! We do that by living according to God's Word.

He said:

Allow me to reiterate that divorce is not the unpardonable sin. God is not done with you, and He still wants to use you. So, we learn from our mistakes, and thereby take what Satan meant for evil and use it for good. (See Genesis 50:20.) I used to be a drug dealer and a drug addict, and now, God uses me to bring drug dealers and addicts out of bondage and into the kingdom of God. Nobody is too far gone.

Preventing Affairs and Avoiding Divorce

Deal with Disappointment

She said:

During a television interview on *I'm Just Sayin'* on Total Christian TV, the host, Pastor Dan Willis, said to me, "I know a lot of couples in the ministry. And, unfortunately, I see so many women who have turned sour and bitter; they're depressed and wounded. It's refreshing to see that you still love the Lord and love people and that you're still excited after thirty-five years in the ministry. How do you stay so fresh, excited, and joyful?" I replied, "Well, Pastor Dan, that's exactly what our next book is all about. That's exactly what Larry and I stand for—every single day, no matter what we face, we have a choice to get bitter or to get better. In our marriages, we have a choice every day to grow closer and to overcome the things that may divide us and get past them, or to grow apart and to get soured and bitter in our lives."

The word *disappointment* indicates an expectation that went unmet. Too many times, men and women enter into marriage with certain expectations. Little girls dream about a knight in shining white armor who's going to come and sweep them off of their feet, and that they're going to ride off into the sunset and live happily ever after. As for you men, I'm not sure what you dreamed about as young boys, but I do know that some of you said "I do" and then woke up the next morning saying "I did?" Disappointment can creep into our marriage, but we don't have to let it stay there.

He said:

In many cases, we depend on the other person to make us happy, never once considering that we may be part of the problem. I see a lot of immature married couples. The husband says, "I want her to make me happy"; the wife says, "I want him to make me happy." I tell them, "Guess what? You need to make yourself happy!" Do it for yourself, as well as for your family, because nobody likes walking on eggshells. If you want to be blessed, be a peacemaker.

The Bible says, *"Blessed are the peacemakers"* (Matthew 5:9). In the home, are we peacemakers or troublemakers? God says, *"I have set before you life and death, blessing and cursing; therefore choose life, that both you and your descendants may live"* (Deuteronomy 30:19). Peacemakers are blessed; troublemakers are cursed. If we want to safeguard our marriage, we need to make sure we are peacemakers rather than troublemakers.

Start with Yourself

It has been said that a person who gets divorced after a marriage of twenty or thirty years and later remarries will probably end up getting divorced again—and then married and divorced again—as many as two or three more times. Do you know why? Because, after someone has been married ten, twenty, or thirty years, and then he or she decides to trade in that thirty for two fifteens, it isn't going to work.

Now, I'm not saying that if you're remarried, your marriage is doomed. But it's important to realize that no matter how many times we might "start fresh" and go after something new, there's no guarantee that our problems won't follow us. We are at least 50 percent responsible for the problems that plague our marriages, including the sense of disappointment we sometimes feel.

If someone were to ask me, "What was the greatest decision you made that contributed to your marriage lasting more than thirty years?" my response would be another question, which changed my life: "How would you like to come home to yourself? Would you want to be married to someone like you?" I came from a broken home and a dysfunctional family; I didn't know how to be the husband or the father God wanted me to be. When I heard someone ask, "How would you like to come home to yourself?" I realized that if I were married to me during the early years of our marriage, I wouldn't come home. Seriously. I was always in a bad mood.

It's easy to recognize the home of an angry man—there's a picture on every wall to hide each of the holes he's punched into them. And an angry woman can be just as bad. She may not be punching holes in the walls, but her tongue alone is capable of inflicting much emotional damage. The Bible compares a quarrelsome wife to a dripping faucet. (See Proverbs 27:15.) You know how irritating it is to lie in bed and hear a faucet leaking: drip, drip, drip—aaaagh! It isn't doing any physical damage, but it just won't stop!

So, that's where we need to start: with ourselves. Sometimes, I'm counseling someone who says, "Pastor, I don't know what happened to make my spouse want to leave me," and I want to say, "I know why, and so does everybody else—you acted like a jerk!" We need to consider ourselves and assess our character. In what ways do we need to mature so that our spouse finds us worth coming home to?

One important step is to go to the Lord in prayer and simply say, "God, change me. Make me the spouse I need to be." Human nature says, "Lord, change him!" or "Lord, change her!" It started back in the garden of Eden, when Adam said, "Lord, it was the woman You gave me who told me to eat the forbidden fruit." (See Genesis 3:12.) We've been blaming each other ever since. But if we say, "Lord, I'm going to lead my spouse to You, if You'll change me and make me into the person I need to be in this marriage," we're on the right track.

Avoid Precarious Positions

She said:

On the episode of *Oprah* I mentioned earlier, marriage expert M. Gary Neuman made another statement that stuck with me: "Don't go looking outside the marriage to fill a void in your heart." There's an attitude in the world that shrugs off searching elsewhere for the fulfillment of needs that you believe your marriage isn't meeting. And it's wrong! That's a slippery slope.

I just was counseling a couple in another state. They're both in their forties, and they've been married for almost twenty years. The wife decided, "I've invested in my children, in my marriage, and all these other things; now, finally, it's my time." So, she made a choice to pursue a certain sporting activity that, to her, seemed harmless. Every evening, rather than being at home with her children, she'd get a babysitter to watch them while she went out and participated in this activity. Time went on, and the activity became increasingly important to her. The people with whom she participated in this activity became more and more important to her, while her family seemed to become less and less so. Eight months later, she and her husband split up because they had nothing left in common.

In many cases, it isn't physical temptation but an emotional connection that draws married people away from their spouses. We need to keep our guard up all of the time, not just at step 7 on a 10-point scale. Let's guard our mind and our heart from square one and refuse to even entertain the idea of a relationship that could prove slippery. Many of those "slippery slope" relationships start at the office. We need to act like professional adults and refuse to play those games! That way, if someone tries to start something with us, we won't reach a point where we find ourselves saying, "I couldn't help myself," because we made that choice the day we said "I do." We made our decision on our wedding day, not the morning of the day when that temptation came on the scene.

Even an emotional affair counts as an affair. We can't afford to go there! Let's not go looking for someone other than our spouse to validate us or to prop up our ego. Instead, let's go to our marriage and build it up so that it is all of the earthly support we could ever need.

Remember, a marriage is like a savings account: we can withdraw only as much as we've invested. We need to invest 100 percent of ourselves. Some people talk about a 50/50 contribution, but that never works. We need to give 100 percent, no matter what. There's a give and take in marriage. Sometimes, one spouse is unable to give 100 percent. Maybe 25 percent is even a stretch. In those cases, the other spouse needs to go the extra mile, be the peacemaker, and pull his or her spouse along. In the seasons of marriage, there may be times when the two spouses grow at different rates. If one spouse pulls ahead in a particular area, he or she needs to bear up the other spouse until he or she catches up.

He said:

It makes me nervous when I hear a Christian man say, "There's my wife—she's my main squeeze." Tiz is not my main squeeze. She's my only squeeze.

I don't flirt—never have, never will. The same thing goes for Tiz. At our church, we have a staff rule that if a male is counseling a female or a female is counseling a male, it's done in an office with the door left open. Either that, or it's done in the presence of another person—no exceptions! In fact, most of the time, I require men to meet with men and women with women. In my thirty-five years of ministry, I've never met a woman for a "counseling lunch." We were pastoring at another church, and I noticed one of the worship leaders—a married man—flirting with a woman from the congregation. When I called him in to talk about it, he confessed that he was in the beginning stages of a secret affair, and he said, "Don't tell my wife. I repent, but please don't tell my wife." I said, "Fine, I will leave that up to you. But you will have to explain it to her, because you're fired." Christians are human, prone to temptation; and flirting can lead to all kinds of sinful behavior. Scripture tells us, "Give no place to the

> *It makes me nervous when I hear a Christian man say, "There's my wife—she's my main squeeze." Tiz is not my main squeeze. She's my only squeeze.*

On the path of marriage, we're always growing, either closer together or further apart. The choice is ours. We can change and grow together in ways that will bless our relationship, or we can change and grow apart in ways that will harm it. Remember, "Today's decisions determine tomorrow's destiny!"

Stay Committed

In today's society, prenuptial agreements are quite common. I'm not saying that they are always a terrible idea, but isn't it sad and a bit strange to make a marriage vow with a built-in escape clause? The Bible says that a double-minded man is unstable in all of his ways. (See James 1:8.) With or without a prenuptial agreement, if we enter into marriage thinking there's a back door of escape, then every conflict will have us running for that back door—for divorce. But if we enter into marriage viewing it as the sacred commitment that it is, and if we commit to each other, come hell or high water, in the good times and the challenging times, we're going to last as a couple. We'll plow through any problems that come our way.

Again, marriage isn't always a bed of roses, even when we marry our soul mate. We're still two separate units—we think differently, process things differently, and so forth. As I said before, even soul mates need to learn how to become roommates!

He said:

In the world, divorce may happen; it happens in the church and, sadly, even in the ministry. There is an epidemic of women leaving their husbands because they aren't spiritual enough, and men leaving their wives because they aren't spiritual enough. "They're blocking my ministry," they say.

I'm not buying it, and I doubt God is, either. It takes a lot of hard work, and sometimes a fight, to make a marriage work. If we aren't willing to fight for our marriage, we may hinder our opportunities to move forward in ministry, because ministry starts at home and then moves outside to the world.

If we love someone enough to say "I do," we ought to be mature enough to do whatever it takes to make our marriage work. Two people who are in the church and who love the Lord need to work on their marriage rather than give up on it at the first sign of trouble.

The Bible instructs us that if we don't have our homes in order, we are disqualified to work in the ministry. (See 1 Timothy 3:5.) Now, I know this is a very touchy subject, and I don't say this lightly, by any means. Please understand that I am not trying to be harsh or to condemn or judge. But I think we are hearing too many excuses and seeing too many marriages failing and falling apart. Life is hard sometimes; I know that. And I've been there, too! Tiz and I went through some incredibly difficult circumstances, and it would have been easy for either of us to throw in the towel. But we stuck it out, pressed through, and persevered. By the grace of God, we made it! We not only survived but thrived. Again, our purpose in writing this book is to set an example and bring hope to other marriages—what the Lord has done for us, He can do for you, too!

One Caveat: Abusive Relationships

I'll never forget the comment of a Christian panelist at a conference I attended years ago: "If you're in an abusive relationship, get out, because we're tired of burying women who are told, 'Just pray.'" If you're in an abusive situation, let's pray, yes, but let's also get you to a place of safety. Nobody has the right to hit anybody else. If someone were to hit my daughters, I would show him a new meaning of the "laying on of hands."

If your spouse is physically abusing you, he or she has departed from the faith. If you're hitting your wife, shame on you. It's time for you to seek help and deliverance. And if you're wife's beating you, join a gym! There are other forms of abuse that are just as dangerous. Any abuse—whether it's physical, mental, emotional, or sexual—is not acceptable behavior, in the context of marriage or anywhere else. Counseling and deliverance are necessary to stop this destructive behavior pattern.

Fight with Faith

She said:

I like to compare marriage to a garden. There are two types of crops in the world—quick crops and long-term crops. Relating this to marriage, some people have marriages that yield a short-term harvest, but it's important to think long-term. When we till the soil of our marriage and say, "No matter what comes our way, we're going to make it through, turning lemons into lemonade," we'll overcome every obstacle and experience exponential growth, or what is called the "law of increased returns." In the banking world, it's called a profit with compound interest. All of a sudden, our growth jumps from slow and steady to sudden and substantial. That's what happens when we commit to building our marriage and family God's way.

We need to make sure that we pray for our spouses and intercede on behalf of our children. I can't tell you how many people come to me asking for prayer for a spouse who is dealing with a major struggle. I am happy to pray, but I always ask, "Have you been praying for your spouse?" Many people respond, "Well, no, I never really thought about praying for him/her." If we don't pray for our families, who will? Husbands and wives need to cover one another in prayer. Moms and dads must cover their children in prayer—every single day, all day long. We wouldn't send our children outside in the rain without the covering of a raincoat, would we? Of course not. And neither should we send them out into the world without the covering of prayer—a spiritual umbrella to protect them from the showers of negative influences and destructive downpours of the enemy.

I'm not trying to make anyone feel guilty. My heart is to encourage and motivate others to take the promises of God and make them theirs. Often, we need to sever the past in order to step into the future. Even if our past was relatively good, we need to cast it off, because "good" is the enemy of "best." Let's not be mediocre. We shouldn't settle for "satisfactory." Let's go after all that God has for us!

Let's raise the standard in marriages. The bar has been lowered more and more over the past several decades. As Christians—those who worship the One who created marriage in the first place—let's set a standard of excellence in marriage.

The only way we fail is if we stop trying. If we fall down six times, that just means we get up seven times. Marriage is a process of continual growth. It's a journey that's filled with challenges, but we are more than conquerors, according to the apostle Paul. (See Romans 8:37.) When we follow the leading of the Lord and allow Him to change us, our marriages will get better with every passing year. It's a series of tiny steps. So, let's give our spouses a little slack. And let's cut ourselves a little slack while we're at it! We can do this. We can create great marriages. Just remember, we're on a journey from glory to glory!

Points to Ponder and Apply

- When we say our wedding vows and pledge our faithfulness to our spouse, we make the same promise to God, and He expects us to keep it. The good news is, we have His divine help and equipping to do just that!

- Divorce is not the "unpardonable sin." It happens, even in the lives of those who follow God. Even if you have been through a divorce, God wants to bless you, bring you joy, and use you to minister to others.

- Popular culture and the media have caused many people to have unrealistic expectations of marriage. Before you go off on your spouse for falling short, ask yourself, "Would I want to come home to me?" If not, then pray that God would show you the steps to take to change for the better, then watch as He transforms you into the person and spouse He wants you to be.

- Don't flirt—ever! Keep that door closed. Watch your emotional ties, so that you may sever any inappropriate relationship before it starts.

- Be willing to change, according to the seasons of life. As you do, stay close to your spouse so that you grow together, not apart.

- There is zero tolerance for abuse! If you or your children are being abused, get out. That doesn't mean divorce, necessarily; it just means get to a safe place. After that, seek help and counsel to know the right course of action.

- Don't settle for quick fixes. Establish a long-term plan and build your family one step at a time.

- Cut each other—and yourself—a little slack! Then, sit back and let God do a work in you and in your marriage.

PART II:

Release Blessings on Your Family and Children

Chapter 6

God's Plan for the Family

You don't choose your family. They are God's gift to you, as you are to them.
—Desmond Tutu

She said:

One of the things nearest and dearest to the heart of God is the family and the home. He established the institution of the family from the beginning of time as a microcosm of what He wanted to do in the world. When the Lord talks about taking dominion in every place we put the soles of our feet, and when He promises that everything we put our hands to will prosper, He means that it starts in the home. God created a master plan, and it works! When we invite His Holy Spirit into our homes, seek His will, keep His commands, and follow His Word, the blessings we receive multiply naturally in to the world.

Yes, God has a heart and a passion for the family. It is His number one priority. He is the Mastermind, the Chief Architect. As the One who designed the family and created it, He alone knows the best way to make it work. The Bible promises us that *"those who are planted in the house of the LORD shall flourish in the courts of our God"* (Psalm 92:13). The word *flourish* means to thrive, grow, bloom, and bear healthy fruit! This is a vivid picture of what God intends for our families to look like when we follow the pattern He established.

Abandoning the Plan

I read a startling article entitled "The Death of the Traditional Family" in the British publication the *Telegram Newspaper*. The author said that women are more likely to give birth before they turn twenty-five than they are to get married. In the author's opinion, this study was a final confirmation that, for the first time in history, more women are getting pregnant before they get married than getting married and then getting pregnant. He concluded that the nuclear family has become a "museum piece." A museum piece? Seriously? Has the family structure slipped that far from the biblical model? It may seem outdated in some circles, but I am convinced that, at the core of every human being, there is a longing and a desire to belong to a tight-knit family.

I believe that there is about to be a resurgence of traditional, "old-fashioned" structures, values, and morals will sweep across the world. People everywhere have tried just about everything to find happiness and "freedom of expression," yet they're still coming up short in the categories of contentment, security, and fulfillment. We need to take another look at the instruction manual provided by the Manufacturer—the Lord God—and get back to the basics laid out in the Bible, which explain how we, as His created beings, and our families are to function.

Recently, I saw an open discussion on the morning news of a new, popular trend in America called "carriage before marriage." The topic was discussed as casually and as matter-of-factly as if they had been talking about the latest trend in women's fashion. "Carriage before marriage" applies to couples who have babies first, before getting married—and many of them never marry at all. This scenario is not new, of course, but the acceptance of it as normal certainly is. Now, I'm not condemning or judging anyone; I'm simply pointing out a problem so that we can work toward finding a solution.

Our modern, liberal world has fallen away from God's plan for the family. It's like the proverbial frog in the pot. If you place a live frog in a pot of cold water on the stove, and then turn up the heat, little by little, he'll never notice, because his body will adjust to the gradual heat change—until he boils to death. And the same thing is happening here in the United States, as well as around the world. The body of Christ is just sitting here passively, on the verge of boiling to death. We need a wakeup call.

Someone said, "The morals of the world can be overturned in one generation." This seems to be an accurate description of what is happening right here, right now, right in front of us. We may not be able to control the morals and values of the entire world, but we can do our best to control the morals and values within our own homes.

I hope that you understand the perspective that Larry and I share, as well as where we're coming from. We have given our entire adult lives to pastoring and counseling people in an effort to restore them to spiritual, emotional, and relational wholeness. More than three decades of pastoring have given us an inside look at the long-term effects of destructive behaviors and dysfunctional patterns in individual relationships and in families. We deal with broken people every day. And while we know that our God heal broken hearts, broken people, and broken families, we think life is a whole lot easier when we can bypass the "breaking" and "repairing" stages—when we "get it right" the first time around.

He said:

The family has departed from God's original blueprint, for sure, and a lot of the blame falls on the fathers. According to ancient Jewish wisdom, the first sign that a people or a nation is cursed is that the sons don't know who their fathers are. I know it's in vogue to be an unwed mother, but that's not biblical. It can be difficult to teach on this because we have so many single parents in the church, but that's the wonderful thing about church—we can help them to get their lives back on course, through youth groups, support groups, counseling, and other programming. Our church is full of all kinds of people with all kind of issues and every type of baggage, yet God loves every one of us. Each of us is a wonderful work in progress!

However, that doesn't negate the need to stop the family curse that comes from or is caused by illegitimate children. If you don't think it's a curse, listen to these alarming statistics:

- 63 percent of teen suicides occur in fatherless homes. That's five times the national average.

- 90 percent of all runaways and homeless children come from fatherless homes. That's thirty-two times the national average.

- 80 percent of rapists come from fatherless homes. That's fourteen times the national average.

- 71 percent of high school dropouts come from fatherless homes. That's nine times the national average.

- 75 percent of adolescent patients in chemical abuse centers come from fatherless homes. That's ten times the national average.

- 85 percent of all those in prison come from fatherless homes. That's twenty times the national average.

- Daughters of single mothers, without the involvement of a father, are 53 percent more likely to become married as teenagers, 71 percent more likely to become teen parents, 16 percent more likely to have premarital births, and 92 percent more likely to get divorced themselves.[3]

I could go on and on, but I've made the point. Again, let me emphasize that I am not pointing this out to condemn or hurt anyone whose circumstances reflect this problem. All of us have made mistakes, and it is only through recognizing them and repenting of them that we can make them right. You are probably familiar with the adage that says, "Those who don't learn from the past are destined to repeat it." As we recognize and repent of the mistakes of our pasts, we can reverse them and see God release His blessings upon our futures! We will talk more about that as we go along.

Back to a Biblical Pattern

She said:

Family life has become a lot more complex and diversified than it was in the 1950s, when I was growing up. The iconic television show *Ozzie and Harriet* was a pretty accurate depiction of the typical family scenario. They would get up in the morning and have breakfast together, and then Ozzie would put on his hat, kiss Harriet good-bye, and leave for the office. Meanwhile, Harriet would stay home to take care of the children, clean the house, and cook dinner. Around five or six o'clock, Ozzie would walk through the door, and they'd kiss again, have dinner together, chat with the kids, read the newspaper, and go to bed. The husband was the breadwinner; the wife was the happy homemaker.

But that's no longer the normal pattern of most marriages. We see single parents raising kids, blended families, families in which Mom and Dad both work, have grandparents raising their grandkids—all kinds of scenarios that were uncommon or unheard of in the days of *Ozzie and Harriet*. Yet, with God, we can still have happy homes and healthy kids. I know a lot of single mothers who have raised wonderful kids completely on their own.

One of our friends got married and had a daughter, only to find herself divorced a short time later. For years, she was a single mom. And then, just last year, she met a wonderful guy and got married again. He is like a dream come true for her—and for her daughter. At the wedding, he knelt down beside her little girl and proclaimed a vow to her, as well: "I take you into my life; you are

---

[3]http://thefatherlessgeneration.wordpress.com/statistics/.

mine." He gave her a little locket containing a photo of them together. God is a restorer!

No matter how many times we mess up or fail to measure up, God will come in and turn it around so that everything works together for good. (See Romans 8:28.) Even if your family portrait looks a little different than you'd imagined it would, God can turn things around and bless you in ways you never thought possible.

At every stage of life, God challenges us to go to an even higher level. If we're really serving Him, He's going to challenge us continually to improve in every area. We must never grow complacent and think that we've made it, or we'll be settling for less than God's best. We may have a great marriage and wonderful children, but God can still do *exceedingly abundantly above all that we ask or think*" (Ephesians 3:20). He can propel us out of mediocrity, which, as I always say, is the best of the worst and the worst of the best. There's always something better in store for us when we're trusting in God and being intentional about improving our relationships.

> *We must never grow complacent and think that we've made it, or we'll be settling for less than God's best.*

It's easy to settle into a rhythm. And that's why God will prompt us to do something to propel our relationship to a higher level, whether it's spending more time with our spouse or taking our kids to the park or doing something else to strengthen our bonds. I'm not saying that you need to take a two-week trip to Maui, believe me! But there are small, simple steps we can take to further our relationships.

Let me give you hope. No matter where your family is or how old your children are, it's never too late to build a family after God's heart. Listen to this letter we received via e-mail.

> Hello,
>
> Here is what God is doing in our lives. We want to praise God for bringing our daughter, her husband, and our two grandchildren, whom we've never seen, back into our lives. They are now ages ten and eleven, we have not seen or had any contact with our daughter for eleven years. She would not speak to us or have anything to do with us. She called and asked if we wanted to see her kids. The best part is, they wanted to go to church with us on Sunday, and so we met them for the first time at

church. How good is God to have a blessed reunion in His house? They were here with us all this week and now have returned home. God is restoring and healing our relationship. What Satan meant for evil, God is reversing the curse and turning it for good. Praise God! Thank you for all your prayers.

God is a good God! Those who are just starting a family can do it the right way—God's way. If we follow God's blueprint, which is laid out in His Word, our family will work out exactly how God wants it to work out. But even if something has happened and there have been some bumps in the road, God can reverse every curse and take what Satan meant for evil and use it for good. (See Genesis 50:20.)

It doesn't matter where we came from; the only thing that matters is where we're going. And the universal fact is that each of us needs to grow and change. So, no matter our background—whether our family is "broken," blended, or whole—God has a beautiful future in store for us, as long as we commit to following His blueprint for the family. Don't be discouraged if your family still needs some work. (What family doesn't?) Rather, be encouraged that you are making progress on the path to positive change. There are some principles that never change, regardless of what our family portrait looks like.

Principle #1: Put Family First

Family is the foundation of our lives, and it should be the most important thing to us, after our relationship with God. This was not always evident to Larry and me. As I said before, when we were first saved, we were part of a fellowship that expected you to sacrifice everything—including your family—for the sake of the ministry. "Your life is not your own" was its creed, and it fostered the notion of God as a hard taskmaster, pushing us harder and harder to win souls for Him. When you're constantly giving of yourself but never receiving, you begin to shut down. Yet that's how we lived. We believed that everything else ought to come before the family, and so we gave our best to the world and saved little to nothing for our own family. We took people in off the streets to live with us. We poured our energies and efforts into hundreds of people, leaving little energy and time for each other and our kids at the end of the day.

We lived like this for fifteen years. Then, an evangelist came to our church and told a story that changed our lives. The story was about a couple in ministry together. One day, the wife came forward and said, "My husband has a mistress." When pressed about the circumstances, she said, "Every time the children or I need attention, the phone rings, and off he goes to the mistress. We need new shoes, new clothes—basic necessities—but there's never any money for our family because he spends all of it on his mistress. He never has time for our family but always has time for his mistress." Who was this mistress? The church. The ministry.

Larry and I just looked at each other and said, "That's what our life has been like all these years." The church had been everything. And the realization was a major turning point in our marriage and family. We started making time for the kids. We began scheduling a day off every week (in theory, anyway). We finally went on vacation! As important as it is to advance the kingdom of God, we were wrong to make it our highest priority. Contrary to what we'd been taught, our family was not a distraction getting in the way of the things of God. It should have been our foundation and our highest priority all along. Praise God, He remedied the situation early enough, and we were able to salvage our relationships with our children and each other.

In our thirty-five years of marriage and ministry, we've traveled the world, pioneering seven churches across the globe, two of them in Australia. We've seen thousands of lives changed by the grace of God. But ask either of us what we consider to be our greatest accomplishment, and we'll say, "Our family." And that family has been the foundation of our ministry, never a roadblock or an obstacle.

Whether we're in the ministry or working another career, our home is to be our top priority. Our professional success will always be an extension of who we are at home. Each Christian household is a miniature church. It's where our character is tested and our traits are developed. That's why the enemy spends so much of his energy attacking our homes. He is bent on destroying the family because he knows how decisive its role is in God's plan to redeem the world.

He said:

Here is some biblical proof of the importance of putting family first. When Moses went to Pharaoh and said, "Let my people go," how did Pharaoh respond? "No," you say? That's true—he said no a couple of times. But then, one time, he said, "Yes, but you can't take the women and children with you." Read with me from Exodus chapter 10:

[Moses delivered a message from God to Pharaoh, saying,] *"Or else, if you refuse to let My people go, behold, tomorrow I will bring locusts into your territory. And they shall cover the face of the earth, so that no one will be able to see the earth; and they shall eat the residue of what is left, which remains to you from the hail, and they shall eat every tree which grows up for you out of the field. They shall fill your houses, the houses of all your servants, and the houses of all the Egyptians; which neither your fathers nor your fathers' fathers have seen, since the day that they were on the earth to this day"* And [Moses] *turned and went out from Pharaoh. Then Pharaoh's servants said to him, "How long shall this man be a snare to us? Let the men go, that they may serve the* Lord *their God. Do you not yet know that Egypt is destroyed?" So Moses and Aaron were brought again to Pharaoh, and he said to them, "Go, serve the* Lord *your God. Who are the ones that are going?" And Moses said, "We will go with our young and our old; with our sons and our daughters, with our flocks and our herds we will go, for we must hold a feast to the* Lord*." Then he said to them, "The* Lord *had better be with you when I let you and your little ones go! Beware, for evil is ahead of you."*   (Exodus 10:4–10)

We lose a lot of the significance in the English translation. When the English Bible says that Egypt is "*destroyed*," the original Hebrew uses the word "doomed." The experts were urging Pharaoh, "We've got to get these children of God out of Egypt, or our country is doomed." And so, Pharaoh finally told Moses to go ahead and leave. But, again, the Hebrew is a little more descriptive. Pharaoh really said, "You *men* go." The implication was that he should leave the women and children behind, because they would slow down the exodus. "Go, build the house of God," Pharaoh said, "and worship God in the desert. But this is God's work, so you should leave the women and children behind."

This Scripture came alive to me due to the buzz that's going around the ministry that says you must be willing to sacrifice your marriage and your family for God's kingdom. Let me be clear: no matter the heart condition of someone who says such a thing, it is absolutely false. God comes first, family comes second, friends come third, and ministry comes last. If you don't have family and you don't have friends and you don't have God, then you really don't have a ministry. We've got it backward. As Tiz explained, when we first went into the ministry, we were expected to sacrifice everything. Thank the Lord we awakened to the truth and pulled out of that fellowship before they were teenagers. We had been sincere, but also sincerely wrong! Our number one ministry is our marriage, family, and home.

In this passage from Exodus, Pharaoh finally relented, on the condition that Moses would leave the women and children behind. Satan knew that if the Israelite men did not take their women and children along with them on their journey, it wouldn't matter what they built; the world was one generation from becoming a godless world. Beware of the wiles of the devil! Men, whether we're building a business or building a ministry, Satan's strategy is to cause us to pour all of our energy into that pursuit, while our wives and children are left wanting our love, attention, and care. They get "left behind" while we forge ahead with our plans for the future. To adapt Mark 8:36, "What will it profit a man if he gains the whole world yet loses his family?" Wouldn't it terrible if I built a church or estab-

> *When we learn to put God first, our families second, and our ministries third, we have everything in order and receive the blessings of God.*

lished a worldwide television ministry, only to lose my wife, my sons, my daughters, and my grandchildren? What would it profit me if I touched the world but I lost my own family?

Now, let's return to our discussion about Moses and the Israelites. Pharaoh told him, "Men, go ahead and go. Go do your thing. Just forget about the women and children." It makes no difference if I'm serving God if my wife and children are not. In my family, God comes first, Tiz comes second, kids come third, friends come fourth, and the ministry comes last. Because, if I lose my family—if I can't pastor my family—how can I pastor my church family?

When we learn to put God first, our families second, and our ministries third, we have everything in order and receive the blessings of God.

Principle #2: Invest Where It Counts

She said:

My mom always reminded my siblings and me, "Thousands of people will come and go in your life, but family is forever." And I've always said the same thing to my own children. Our families are the people we should value above everyone else because family relationships are not temporary. They're forever. So, we may as well make them the best they can be! The truth is, family needs to be a priority for us. We need to make it important, not just in theory, but in practice.

If I go to the bank and try to withdraw $10,000 from my account, but my balance is only $5,000, I'm not going to receive $10,000. I can withdraw only as much as I've invested (unless I've earned interest, but that's beside the point).

There's no closer parallel than in the family. If we give minimal commitment, we're going to get minimal commitment in return. But, if we commit fully, we're going to receive full commitment. Not only that, but God will multiply all of our efforts for the good of our family and our marriage.

Let's make a conscious effort to deposit generously in the "bank" of our family relationships, whether those deposits are of an emotional, physical, or mental nature. If we will do that, God will breathe His breath of life into our families, and the results will be transformed lives, as well as a transformed world.

Invest Time

You've probably heard it said that "love" is spelled T-I-M-E. We say we love our children; we say that we care about them. But let's take a look at our schedule and evaluate the amount of time we really commit to them. How important are they, really?

We can say that we love God, but if we never spend time with Him, in prayer and in Bible study, do we really love Him? The same question applies to our families. We can tell our kids and our spouses that we love them, but if we never make time for them, our relationship is going to deteriorate. We have to make time for those things that are important to us, even as countless other things scream for our attention.

I'm just like you. There are a million things demanding my attention in any given week. And so, I have to decide in my heart that I'm going to set aside quality time to spend with my husband, my kids, and my grandkids. Larry and I have explained that when we first got saved, we were part of a group that demanded allegiance to the ministry above allegiance to one's family. One pastor even said that if we had time to take a vacation, we weren't working hard enough for God! And so, for fifteen years of marriage and ministry, we never set aside time to have fun together. It was work, work, work. Praise God, we're getting paid back now! But that teaching was erroneous. We now understand that, number one, the Sabbath is a day every week that's appointed for us not only to honor God but also to experience refreshment and renewal, as God pours out His blessings onto us and our families after a week's worth of labor.

My kids are grown, but they still say, "Mom, Dad, we've got to spend some time together." But life is busy, and, the next thing we know, it's been a week or even a month since we've actually gotten together and spent time as a family. Life is too short to miss out on opportunities to spend time together. Most people, when they reach the end of their earthly lives, say that they regret not having spent more time with their families, with the people they love. So, even if we have a wonderful marriage and a fantastic family, there's always room for growth. Each of us is a work in progress, just as our families are.

Invest Energy

Sometimes, other people seem to think you aren't doing your job if you aren't worn ragged every minute of the day. If you're a pastor, like Larry and I, you're expected to be on the job 24/7, visiting someone in the hospital, counseling someone over the phone, and so forth. It took years for us to figure out that God wanted us to put our family first. The idea that pastors must sacrifice their families for the sake of the ministry is bogus. No matter our calling, the enemy will fight you. For those of us who love God, whether we're behind the pulpit or in the pews, the devil opposes all efforts toward the family. But we don't have to forsake our families in order to find success in the ministry, in business, or in anything else! Our home is the most important place in the world, and our family members are the most important people in the world, because the home—the family—is where world change begins.

> *Let's not shortchange our families because we've spent all our energy serving the world.*

Of course, we want to be a blessing to the world, but let's not forget to be a blessing at home! Some days, we go to the office, work hard all day, and give it our best, only to return home and crash. We just want to chill. We've spent all day being a blessing; we don't want to be a blessing to everybody in our house. We want someone else to cook dinner for us, to take care of us, to wait on us hand and foot. But our family is supposed to be our first priority, remember? Instead of giving our best to the world and then coming home with scraps of leftovers for our families, let's make sure to give our best to the world and then amp it up for the family. Let's not shortchange our families because we've spent all our energy serving the world.

There are a lot of pressures and demands on all of us. But God will equip us, strengthen us, and give us the wisdom, knowledge, and help we need. He'll apply His "super" to our "natural" when we make a commitment to our families.

Now, dads and moms, this means that you need to save some of your energy. Ration it throughout the day. Disengage a little from the chaos at work when you come home at the end of the day.

Invest Quality Conversation

A recent study determined that, on average, a parent engages in "meaningful conversation" with his kids about 3.5 minutes per week.[4] Of course, "meaningful conversation" does not include casual greetings when your paths cross in the house. So, if your interactions with your children are limited to that, it doesn't count. How often do we really talk with our kids one-on-one? How frequently do we ask them open-ended questions, such as, "How is the world treating you this week?" "What's going on at school?" "How is your latest project going?" "How are your friends doing?"

Engaging conversation is key! If we really talk to our kids no more than two and a half minutes each week, pretty soon, a week turns into a month, a month turns into two months, and two months turns into a year. The next thing we know, our kids have progressed to the next grade level in school, and we're left wondering what they did in the past year. We may be able to say that we made it through the year without any major family drama or chaos, but there's much more to life than simply skating through. It's important to set goals regarding our relationships with our kids, so that we can see measurable results in their lives at the end of each year.

We need to find some common ground. Between taxiing our children to and fro, packing their lunches, and tucking them into bed, surely, we can fit in more than just two minutes of conversation a week. Our kids need to connect with us on a deeper level. They need to hear us say more than just, "I'll pick you up at three" and "What would you like in your lunch today?" We need to have the type of conversations that build relationships. We need to model our interactions with our kids so that they stand out. We need to put forth the effort to break down the barriers that divide.

---

[4]http://www.csun.edu/science/health/docs/tv&health.html.

I read a story recently about a little boy who met his father at the door one evening as he returned home from work and asked him, "Daddy, how much money do you make an hour?"

The father replied, "What kind of crazy question is that?"

"I just want to know, Daddy."

"Son, that is a rude question, and it's none of your business. Go to your room."

After some time, the father went to the boy's bedroom and found him sobbing into his pillow. He sat down beside him and tried to console him, asking, "What is this all about? Why are you asking me these questions?"

The little boy replied, "Daddy, I didn't mean to be rude to you. It's just that I hardly get to spend any time with you anymore." He pointed to his open piggy bank and said, "I thought that I could give you the amount of money you make in an hour so that you could take an hour of your time with me."

Sobering, isn't it? Life is busy and hectic; it goes by so fast. Before we know it, days turn into weeks, weeks turn into months, months turn into years, and we've allowed those people we love and those things that are important to us to be pushed to the back burner. Let's make a point to spend more time and effort on those we love—before it's too late.

Principle #3: Find a Church Family to Lean On

One key to bring blessings on our marriage and our family is by being a part of a church family and serving God together with all our heart. From thirty-three-plus years of marriage, I can tell you that you're going to encounter some rocky spots. There are going to be some issues that we'll have to resolve, some mountains we'll have to bring low, and some personality conflicts we'll have to work through. But when we serve the Lord together, all of those issues become small and manageable.

This is how Larry and I made things work. In all of our years of marriage, we have always put God first. And we've never missed church, at least voluntarily. (There have been times when illness has kept us at home.) The blessing truly comes from serving God wholeheartedly and remaining faithful to His bride, the church.

Almost all of us have fought on the way to church. But then, when it's time to head home again, we've been reminded that you serve a greater cause than whatever we were arguing about earlier. The Bible says that those who plant themselves in the house of the Lord will flourish. (See Psalm 92:13.) Let's plant ourselves in the church! Let's plant our children in the church, too. What a difference it would make if people were as committed to getting their kids to church as they were to getting them to soccer practice or ballet lessons. Those activities are good, of course, but not when they take precedence over church involvement, or when parents make every effort to get their kids to those activities and then sit back and say, "Oh, they can miss church this Sunday."

I know a woman whose five-year-old daughter has karate class at 6:00 p.m., five nights a week. This woman and her husband juggle their schedules, taking turns to rush home, pick up their daughter, and whisk her off to practice. Quite a commitment, isn't it? People exhibit such commitment to the things of this world, but then, when it comes to the things of God, such as church attendance, they say, "Feel free to stay home, honey; you have homework to do, and I know that you're tired, so you don't have to go to the service." Some people insist that they can serve God and have a relationship with Him without regular church attendance. To those people, I say, "Sure, but it'll make your parenting job a lot more challenging!" The way that seems right to a man or woman may just be a path leading to destruction. (See Proverbs 14:12.) We can't develop our relationship with God in a vacuum; it must be cultivated in a community of fellow believers. Let's change the world, one family at a time.

> *A church nurtures our spiritual growth and gives us fertile soil in which to invest as a family. It also provides a place for people to connect and be involved, especially when former grounds of connection are gone.*

Being involved with a church family further strengthens our natural family. It provides us with a network of brothers and sisters in Christ—a body of believers to uphold and support us through thick and thin. A church nurtures our spiritual growth and gives us fertile soil in which to invest as a family. It also provides a place for people to connect and be involved, especially when former grounds of connection are gone—such as when all of the kids have left the nest. Empty nesters have a high divorce rate because the husband and wife reach the conclusion of, "Now that the kids are gone, we have nothing left to talk about. We've got nothing in common anymore." To keep their marriages strong, Christian couples need to plug into a church, where they can share a common focus.

Of course, they won't be immune to the enemy's attacks. I'm speaking from experience when I say that he'll try to get you to fight on the way to church. If we give in and fall into this trap, it will block our hearts from receiving the Word of God during the service, because harboring iniquity and unforgiveness creates an impenetrable barrier. If we come to church with a bad attitude, it will take more than the length of the service to get ourselves pumped up enough to focus on the Word of God. Believe me, I've been there! I've sat there, stewing and stressing over what I should have said or how I should have responded, instead of yielding my heart to God in worship and praise. That's how the enemy's strategy works. But he doesn't stop there! He tries to get us to fight the moment we step outside the church door.

This used to happen to Larry and me all the time. We'd walk in our house after the Sunday morning service, and there would be a spirit of contention in the air—a spirit of division. And we'd start fighting. Remember James 4:7: *"Resist the devil and he will flee from you."* My friend Margaret likes to say, "You can't determine whether the birds fly over your head, but you can determine whether they make a nest in your hair." Thoughts will come into our mind out of nowhere, it seems, but we don't have to let them stay. We can choose to take the high road—to live out the Word. Let's refuse to dwell on the garbage the devil sends our way. It's no fun wallowing in self-pity!

One day, Larry and I finally decided that we were tired of fighting and arguing. We said, "We're married now. Let's act like adults." Guess what? We both changed because (1) we decided to, and (2) we looked to God to change us.

There have been times when I honestly think that if it hadn't been for coming to church, I would have been mad for an entire week over a silly little argument. We put on a "church face," and it changes us from the outside in. It's like when a woman said to a little girl, "My, your mama has a pretty smile," and the little girl said, "Oh, that's Mama's church face." It's okay to put it on! At least it's a place to start. When we come into the house of God, we wear a smile and stay on our best behavior, don't we? Well, if we can do it in church, then we can keep it up when we go out into the world. Let's put on our "church face" in the car, at home, at work, and everywhere else. If the enemy steps in and tries to steal our joy, we can stand firm and refuse to let him. Let's wear that smile like it's our last piece of clothing!

You, Too, Can Have a "Fabulous, Forever" Family

Maybe your family consists of a single mom and two kids. Maybe your home is not what you would consider the "perfect" family unit. Whatever your situation, God has promised to bless you and show you how to build a strong family that lasts. If you've made mistakes in the past—and who hasn't?—remember that we serve a God of second chances. He is a God of redemption and restoration.

Many people are haunted by guilt over mistakes they've made, especially regarding the "things that count," such as their families. Guess what? That's where God really shines! He is an expert at taking broken vessels and repairing them, so that they're as good as new. Everything the enemy has stolen, God will give back to us, above and beyond what we originally had.

We don't have to settle for the same mistakes the world makes. There are countless opinions in the world on how to raise our kids, on how to have a good marriage, and so forth. But we care only about the opinion of God, our heavenly Father, because He designed us and knows what we must do to have fabulous, forever families. It's never too late!

To illustrate this truth, let me share a beautiful story about a great leader named Rabbi Yisroel Salanter. Late one evening, Rabbi Yisroel brought his shoes to a shoemaker to be repaired. The cobbler's workshop was illuminated by the final flickers of a candle that was beginning to burn out. "It's a pity," said Rabbi Yisroel, "you won't have time to complete the repair."

"Don't worry, Rabbi," the shoemaker answered. "As long as the candle burns, there is still time for repairs."

"What an incredible thought!" Rabbi Yisroel exclaimed.

Rocking back and forth, he began to sing the melody he used to study ethical works: "As long as the candle of the soul burns, there is still time to mend our ways."

No matter what our family's condition may be, it is never too late to mend our ways and to bring healing into our homes. Today can be your new beginning, with new opportunities and fresh help from the Lord. Let's begin a new chapter as we rewrite the story of our lives and our families so that they align with God's plan. We may not be able to rewrite the pages of our past, but the future is an endless stream of blank pages waiting to be filled with the blessings of God for our lives and our families.

Points to Ponder and Apply

- The family is God's chosen conduit to get His blessings to the world.

- Marriage and family are a two-person assignment.

- God is a restorer, and He has a plan to bless us, no matter what we have done or what shape our marriage is in.

- Don't sacrifice your family for anything, even your ministry. In fact, your first ministry should be your family.

- Invest time, energy, and creativity into your family. Spending a special day together doesn't require that you spend a lot of money.

- God blesses us so that we might be a blessing to others.

- Getting connected with a local church family is vital for family health.

- Release the spirit of unity in your home. Refuse to allow divisions to prevail.

Chapter 7
Positive, Purposeful Parenting

The trouble with being a parent is that by the time you are experienced, you are unemployed.
—Author Unknown

He said:

We try to take a family vacation once a year. Life passes so quickly, and we realize how easy it is to miss out on spending those special times together. It's always a challenge to take time off for the vacation, but if we don't make the time, we miss out. For one particular family vacation, we rented a house at a nearby lake. (Actually, due to a lack of rain, the lake was pretty much non-existent.) We spent the whole week together, all in one place. As we were getting ready to pack up and come home, my grandsons, the twins, said, "Sabba, can we ride in your truck?" And so we put their car seats in my pickup truck for the drive home. Then, as we were arriving in Dallas, they said, "Can we stay the night at your house?" I thought to myself, *It doesn't get any better than this. We've been together for a week, and still they want to stay with us!* A family that finds joy in spending time together is part of God's original plan. By the grace of God, that's what we've enjoyed.

Now, the challenge in teaching on this subject is to avoid making people feel bad. I'm not out to make anyone feel guilty. No parent has done everything completely right! I believe John Wilmot, the second Earl of Rochester, got it right when he said, "Before I got married, I had six theories about bringing up children. Now, I have six children, and no theories." Especially in today's society, it's a hard job being a parent. I, for one, find it especially difficult to be the type of father I'm supposed to be: strong and sensitive, brave and tender, protector and cuddler. Some of those things aren't natural to us men, not to mention that they seem paradoxical! It's a tough balance being a husband and a father. We see male sex symbols on television, but they're never out there digging a ditch or loading up a truck or building a church. We don't see them in real activities of life, the daily routine. We don't see them working a job in the real world. It's a hard job being a man and working a job, but it's necessary.

She said:

I once saw an ad for a boys and girls club I found extremely effective. It featured a photo of a Jell-O mold filled with plastic toy animals. The headline read something along the lines of, "Kids are like Jell-O. You've got to get all the good stuff in before it hardens." If you've ever made Jell-O, you know that once you add water and stir to dissolve the mix, it's only a matter of time before the mold sets and solidifies, so to speak. If you want to set something in the Jell-O, such as pieces of fruit or even plastic toys, you need to add them when the Jell-O is still in liquid form. In the same way, we've got to get the "good stuff"—godly teachings, biblical wisdom—into our kids before their hearts harden and become impenetrable.

The High Calling of Parents

We really do have such a small window of opportunity to shape our kids—to love them unconditionally, to teach them how to love unconditionally, to impart manners and how to be polite, to teach them life skills, to impart manners and respect, to give them a place to practice sharing and cooperating. To help them discover their talents and develop them. As their parents, we're their first audience, and our homes are where they make their debut performance in whatever their skill may be. We have a brief portal of time to nurture their creativity and inspire their dreams; to instill values, set boundaries, establish traditions, and shape their worldview.

Our mission on the earth is to heal a broken world—*tikkun olan*, in Hebrew. One of the most important ways we do this is through our kids, by teaching them and equipping them to join in our efforts to bring healing and wholeness to the world.

Raising Children Who Heal the World

I read a book written by a woman whose mother had survived the Jewish Holocaust and gone on to become a rabbi. Today, she and her husband are the rabbis of a synagogue in New York. A major topic of the book was how to raise children with a soul. The author wrote how, when her mother had been released after the Holocaust, she'd decided that her life's mission would be to do whatever she could to bring hope and healing to the world. So, at a young age, she began to look for ways to bring joy to the world—good deeds she could do to heal the broken world, one bit at a time. And as she reached out in love, doors opened.

Today, this woman and her husband have a worldwide presence through their teachings, but they practice the same commitment to good deeds in their household, where the process starts and multiplies. As I like to say, if it isn't working at home, don't export it. But if it's working at home—if it's proven itself—then, by all means, take it into all the world, so that it multiplies exponentially.

Teaching by Example

The Word tells us to *"train up a child in the way he should go, and when he is old he will not depart from it"* (Proverbs 22:6). *"Train up a child"* does not mean "Bark orders at him" or "Tell your kids, 'Do as I say, not as I do.'" Training up our children implies that we set an example of serving God and loving Him with all of our hearts. It means having a vibrant relationship with God that spills over into our relationships with our kids. It isn't enough to merely teach. We need to live out the same things so that our actions reinforce our words. Remember, we teach what we know, but we reproduce who we are. If we think our kids aren't listening to us, we should guess again. They don't miss a beat. We need to watch what we say.

> *Training up our children means having a vibrant relationship with God that spills over into our relationships with our kids.*

Instilling Morals and Values

The Torah calls the foundation of the family the "image of the father," or *deyukno shel aviv*. In other words, embedded in the hearts of all God's children is the image and voice of the father—their heavenly Father and also their forefathers, or the founders of our faith. It also means their earthly fathers and mothers, who set an example and taught them how to live. Their example becomes embedded in their children as their moral compass—a pattern that multiplies and self-propagates.

I heard a man put it like this: "When my children were born, I looked at them as blank CDs, and I realized I wanted to be the voice that was recorded on their life CD." Now, we can't completely isolate our children from all other influences. Most of us don't want to live like monks on a remote mountaintop somewhere.

But we need to make sure that the positive influences outweigh the negative ones. We need to make sure that we have strong, solid relationships with our families, so that our children won't even desire what the world has to offer. And this happens when we build within them a moral fiber based on the Word of God—when we give them a moral compass that helps them navigate the world with wisdom.

Setting the Bar High

He said:

As we've established, parents have a very short window of time in which to mold and shape their children. Did you know that the designation of "teenager" didn't come around until the early 1940s? Up to that point, in every culture, one went from being a child to becoming an adult. And so, when labor laws necessitated a different distinction for those between the ages of thirteen and nineteen, we basically gave each person a built-in eight-year vacation. For many, the teenage years are just one long party, during which minimal effort is necessary. That is ungodly! We shouldn't be paralyzed by a desire for our kids to enjoy themselves. Of course, we want them to have fun, but not at the expense of their future. We want to put them on a path of integrity, accountability, and discipline. We need to establish patterns that will enable them to succeed in life.

Unfortunately, countless parents are allowing their teenage children to enter adulthood completely unprepared for the road ahead, all because they didn't want to be "too hard" on them. There are no free rides! It's a tough world out there. No one can afford to slack off during the teenage years, earning C's when he's capable of A's. No one can afford to do the bare minimum at school or in a job. When we expect our children to do their best, they will rise to the occasion and reach—even exceed—their potential. But let's make sure we validate them and their efforts. One way is by practicing what Tiz likes to call "praise phrases." From the time they are little, it's important to tell them, "Good job!" "I'm proud of you!" "You're doing great."

As parents, grandparents, and pastors, we are keenly aware of the powerful, positive effects of building self-esteem and confidence into our family members. Conversely, we are also keenly aware of the powerful negative effects that result when we tear others down and deflate their self-esteem.

Six Keys to Effective Parenting

She said:

Our daughter Katie gave me an interesting book called *Mother Nurture: Life Lessons from the Mothers of America's Best and Brightest*. It was written by Stephanie Hirsch, a woman who started having children only to find herself desperately wondering how to raise them to be high achievers without pushing them too hard, too fast. She started asking herself questions, such as, "How many hours of television should I allow my kids to watch per day?" "Should I push them to participate in sports, or just sit back and let them join if they want to?" "Say they take up a sport. If they get tired and want to quit, do I push them to keep it up, anyway, or do I encourage them to explore a different area?"

Every parent struggles with questions like these. And the Bible doesn't have specific answers to these types of questions, which can add to our concerns. God's Word gives us the groundwork for parenting but offers no explicit instructions for many of our specific questions and everyday decisions. At this point, it's wise to consult other parents who have raised good, godly kids, as well as to realize that while the Bible contains certain absolutes, there are also countless areas in which we need to figure things out on our own—areas where there's no clear sense of right and wrong.

Finally, the author decided to interview the mothers of some of the world's highest achievers—people who have made a mark on this world, thereby leaving it in a better condition than that in which they found it. And so, Stephanie Hirsch interviewed the mothers of Steven Spielberg, Alicia Keys, Cindy Crawford, Diane Sawyer, Matt Lauer, Derek Jeter, and Tim McGraw, among others, in an effort to figure out what these women did right to raise such standout kids.

While every mother's story was unique, there were several currents of consistency that I want to mention for those of you navigating the tumultuous waters of parenthood. Of course, I am not necessarily vouching for these women's spiritual influence in the lives of their children; my mission is merely to examine their overall influence, Christian values aside.

Key #1: Offer Unconditional Support

First of all, Steven Spielberg's mother, Leah Adler, said that it was no surprise her son had turned out the way he did; he'd spent his entire childhood and adolescence making movies in the backyard with her old video camera. She said that she never had any great aspirations for him—she never said to herself, *My son is going to be a world-famous producer and director*—but she was able to acknowledge his passion and gift for movie-making, as well as how much he enjoyed it. And so she supported him all the way.

At twelve years old, Steven asked her to drive him to the desert so that he could make a movie on the desert flora and fauna. So, she agreed, and they camped in the desert for a few days while he made a movie. Thanks to his mother's fostering of his passion, Steven had produced movies that were being viewed all over the world by the time he was fifteen. One statement by Ms. Adler that struck me was that "my part in this was letting him direct me." She added, "I schlepped him wherever he went." *Schlepped* is Yiddish term, and she was basically saying, "I took him wherever he needed to go." She acted as a facilitator of his talents and passions, and that's a big part of our job as parents: to observe and encourage the abilities and affinities we see in our children. We need to notice their potential and help them discover it for themselves.

Key #2: Bring Out the Best in Your Children

Almost every one of the moms interviewed said she'd noticed a passion in the life of her son or daughter and had nurtured it along the way. They'd worked to bring out the greatness in their children, and an almost universal sentiment was that you will succeed and find happiness if you do what you love.

Along the same lines, these mothers stressed the importance of paying attention to their children's interests. A lot of the time, this process involves trial-and-error. Some kids will try anything and everything, and it's up to us, as parents, to pick up on their particular giftings, and then to help cultivate those aptitudes.

Many of these mothers also mentioned the powerful impact of exposing their children to a higher level of their interests. For example, if your children like to paint and draw, take them to a museum and show them the works of those who are masters in the arena of art. If they're active in sports, take them to a game, let them talk to a professional athlete, and otherwise introduce them to the aspects of an athletic career. If their skill is in music, take them to see a performance by a symphony orchestra, a jazz band, or another professional ensemble.

When I was a little girl, I loved to draw, but I was shy and embarrassed about showing my artwork to anyone else. I didn't think highly of my skills. I will never forget the day when my mom came home from work with a special gift for me. I was about seven years old at the time. As I was opening the bag, she said to me, "I know how much you love to draw. You have such an eye and a gift for art! So, I bought you a set of drawing books, drawing pads, and pencils. Now, you can really express yourself!" I can still feel the explosion of confidence her words ignited within me at that moment. Her investment of encouragement validated my sense of self-worth and fueled an artistic talent that has stayed with me to this day.

Starting at age one, our son, Luke, would pick up a broom, a stick, or whatever was handy and pretend it was a guitar. It was obvious that he had a passion for music. And we tried to encourage this passion as best we could. From the time he was in grade school through today, at thirty years of age, he has been involved in our church in the areas of music, media production, and worship. When he expressed interest in becoming a youth pastor, we sent him to national conferences, where he gained exposure to various methods and approaches to ministry. All of these investments have helped him to grow, flourish, and excel in the giftings and callings that the Lord placed within him.

It can sometimes be somewhat of an inconvenience to take our kids to these various events, but if we want them to succeed, we need to do all we can to facilitate their growth in their areas of giftedness. Having said that, let me add that I don't mean we have to incorporate activities to the point where they become burdensome. Here is the motto I have always used to balance our family's schedule: "We can do and be everything in life that we want to; we just can't do it all at the same time!" Life gets busy, and its constant demands—from school activities to sports, from community involvement to church commitments—can push us to the point of exhaustion. We have to maintain a balance in order to avoid wearing ourselves out. Larry and I have always based our decisions on our long-term goals for our family, which always helps us to organize our priorities in a sensible way.

It sounds easy on paper, doesn't it? Every family has to sort out the path, the priorities, the commitments and the purposes for their own lives. When we implement God's biblical priorities first, the rest falls into place much more easily.

Key #3: Expect Great Things of Your Children

There are occasions when firm discipline is called for, and we will address those occasions in a later chapter. But it's possible to make the majority of our discipline and guidance gentle, as in positive reinforcement. When a child comes home with a C, and his mother knows he was capable of an A—he just needed to put forth more effort—she doesn't have to beat the fire out of him. She simply should tell him that the grade is not acceptable because she knows he can do better. Our goal should be to produce positive self-esteem in our kids, wherever they are, as we also motivate them to achieve their best.

I read an interview with one of the wealthiest people in America, who happens to be a woman. She was on the cover of a leading business magazine. Her name is Sara Blakely, and she invented a line of undergarments called Spanx. In the interview, she explained how she had faced tremendous obstacles and failures in her past but had kept on learning from her mistakes and pressing forward. She shared how, while she was a young child, her father shaped her attitude toward life—an attitude that translated into foundational principles of success for her adult life. Every evening at dinner, her father would ask her and her siblings this question: "How did you fail today, and how are you going to learn from it and fix it?" Each child was expected to answer the question in detail. Ms. Blakely emphasized that her father's attitude was not condescending or demeaning; it was illuminating and thought-provoking. He taught his children how to turn every failure into a life lesson to help them become successful, productive, and independent.

Let's train our children to look at life not through a lens of defeat and failure but through a lens that views every challenge as an exciting opportunity for potential growth.

I call this method "failing forward"! In life, we will always encounter challenges, but, thanks to our heavenly Father's equipping, we are *"more than conquerors"* (Romans 8:37), and we can overcome them! Let's train our children to look at life not through a lens of defeat and failure but through a lens that views every challenge as an exciting opportunity for potential growth. Let's also make sure we express our confidence in their ability to overcome every challenge! When we expect the best from our children, we push them toward greatness. As Lady Bird Johnson once said, "Children are likely to live up to what you believe of them."

He said:

In 1 Corinthians 13:11, the apostle Paul wrote, *"When I was a child, I spoke as a child, I understood as a child, I thought as a child; but when I became a man, I put away childish things."* He made the jump from child to man without any mention of a middle period, which we now call "adolescence." The first time the word *teenager* was used was in an issue of *Reader's Digest* from 1941. In many other cultures, a child makes the transition to adulthood at the age of thirteen. That's why the apostle Paul said, "I acted like a child in childhood, and then—boom!—I became a man and started acting like one."

I went online and did a search to see what the so-called experts tell us we can reasonably expect from our children when they become teenagers, and some of the things I found included make their beds, take phone messages and write them down, clean up their rooms (with help from Mom or Dad), and perform one daily chore. Of course, there was a disclaimer that said something along the lines of, "These expectations come from a physiologist; don't expect them to be able to do all of these things." If we expect too little of our teenagers, "too little" is what we'll get; their performance will never improve to a higher level. But our teenage children are not teenagers of the world—they're teenagers in the family of God, and He expects greatness from them.

I read a compelling book called *Do Hard Things: A Teenage Rebellion against Low Expectations*. It was written by twin brothers, Alex and Brett Harris. The Harris brothers were raised in a Christian home, and, when they were seventeen, they started doing outreach over the Internet. They said, "This is written for teenagers, by teenagers." Recalling a time before "teenager" was even a word, they wrote about three people: first, a man named George who was born to a middle-class family in northern Virginia in 1732. When he was eleven years old, he lost his father. His peers never considered him to be very bright, but he applied himself to his studies and mastered geometry, trigonometry, surveying, algebra, and calculus by the time he was sixteen. (If he had lived in our day, I think he would have been capable of doing a lot more than answering the phone and taking a message.) At seventeen years of age, George had the chance to put his studies to use in his first job as an official surveyor for a county in Virginia. This was no job for a boy, and it certainly wasn't mere busywork. For the next three years, George endured the hardships of frontier life as he measured and recorded previously unmapped territories using heavy log chains as his tools. George became a man, and was paid a man's wages, at the age of seventeen.

David was born in 1801 near the city of Knoxville, Tennessee, where his father was serving in the state militia. At ten years old, David began a career at sea, serving as a naval cadet on the warship *Axis*. At eleven, he saw his first battle. At twelve, David was given command of a ship that had been captured in battle, and he was dispatched with a crew to take the vessel and its men back to the United States. On the journey home, the captive British captain took issue at being ordered around by a twelve-year-old, and he announced that he was going below to get his pistols. (Out of respect for his position, he had been allowed to keep them.) David promptly sent him word that if he stepped on the deck with his pistols, he would shoot him and throw him overboard. The captain never came back on deck.

The third person was named Clara. She was born in Oxford, Massachusetts, on Christmas Day 1821. She was the baby of the family, and her next sibling was ten years older than she. As a child, Clara was timid and so terrified of strangers that she was often barely able to speak. Then, something happened that would change her life forever. When she was eleven years old, her brother David fell from the barn roof and was seriously injured. Young Clara was frantic and begged to be allowed to help care for him. In her brother's recovery room, Clara surprised everyone by demonstrating skills and experience beyond her years. She learned how to take the best care of her brother, until, finally, the doctor allowed her to take full responsibility for his medical care for the remainder of his recovery, which lasted two more years. One year later, at age fourteen, Clara became the nurse of her father's hired man who had come down with smallpox. She soon treated more patients as the smallpox epidemic spread through Massachusetts. She was still shy and timid, but her desire to serve others drove her to overcome her fear. By age seventeen, she was a successful schoolteacher with a classroom of forty students, many of whom were nearly as old as she.

At the end of these stories, we learn that George was none other than George Washington, the first president of the United States. David was David Farragut, the first admiral of the United States Navy. And Clara was Clara Barton, who founded the American Red Cross. The point is that young people are capable of great things when we expect great things of them.

The world is telling us, "You can expect your teenage children to take out the trash or to do the dishes, but not to do both." The world calls us tyrants if we ask our kids to do "more than they can handle." But our teenage children are not children of the world! They have been destined by God for greatness. Moreover, Lamentations 3:27 says, *"It is good for a man to bear the yoke in his youth."* In other words, what makes him a man is the formative years—his youth. We shouldn't set our expectations as low as the world's. Let's expect our children to be what God wants them to be—young men and women who are destined for greatness.

The apostle Paul wrote to his mentor Timothy and said, *"Let no one despise your youth, but be an example to the believers in word, in conduct, in love, in spirit, in faith, in purity"* (1 Timothy 4:12). He was saying, in essence, "Don't let anybody tell you you're too young to be used greatly by God. Show them what you can do. You may be young, but you're a child of God, handpicked by Him to change the world forever."

> *Let's expect our children to be what God wants them to be— young men and women who are destined for greatness.*

We live in one of the greatest countries in the world—a nation that was built on a foundation of faith in God. In order to keep it great, we have an obligation to train up our children in the way they should go. When the devil comes around and whispers, "You're being too strict," or "Don't expect too much from your children," let's put him in his place! Many of the children in other nations are turning into world leaders in the realms of science, technology, medicine, and so forth, while the children of America are falling behind—due to in large part to their parents' backpedaling. We do our children a disservice when we allow them to settle for mediocrity. We should love our kids regardless of their performance, but we should also encourage them to strive for their fullest potential.

Teenagers, you are the future. When Mom and Dad are telling you no— when your parents say, "Be home by this time," "Don't hang out with so and so," "Here's what you can do, and here's what you can't"—it's not because they're mean or because they don't want you to have any fun. It's because they love you so much, it hurts. You are the ones we're passing the mantle to, and you are not destined to fail. You are destined for greatness. You are called to change the world.

Key #4: Don't Be Too Democratic

Years ago, when we pastored a church in Portland, Oregon, a family approached me and said that they wanted me to teach a particular subject in our services. I didn't agree with their point of view, and I said so, but I assured them I would pray about it. They said, "Don't you think you ought to bring it before the church and take a vote?" And I said, "What?" Again, they said, "Don't you think you ought to take it to the people and put it to a vote?" Leaders don't ask for a vote when they are called to lead. Sheep don't tell the shepherd where to take them to eat; they go where they are being led. A leader leads. He asks for input and direction, but he doesn't put the big decisions to a vote. God places leaders where He wants them, and His system is meant to eliminate unnecessary chaos and to streamline success!

Now, if we'd been trying to settle something as simple as the color we ought to order for the new carpet for the sanctuary, we would have gotten several hundred different responses. This couple told me, "In our family, we vote on everything." Their kids were probably ten and eleven years old. While I understand the wisdom in including kids on certain decisions, it isn't wise to leave it to a ten-year-old to determine household policies. Yet, every day, we see eight-year-olds bossing their moms and dads around. The whole thing is upside-down! Along with the wonderful privileges of parenting comes a tremendous responsibility to teach our kids that the Word of God is nonnegotiable. We can't take a vote to determine what to believe and what to cast off as "archaic" or unpleasant.

I can't help but imagine Jesus at the wedding feast in Cana of Galilee. He was probably feeling pretty good about Himself. He knew He was the Son of God. He knew He would change the world. Then, His mother, Mary, came to Him and said, "They need more wine!" And Jesus responded, "*Woman, what does your concern have to do with Me? My hour has not yet come*" (John 2:4). I can picture Mary raising her eyebrows, as mothers do, cocking her head, and saying, "Excuse me? What did You just say to me? Who do You think You are? You may be the Son of God, but, in this house, You are the Son of Mary, and when I tell You to help out, You help out!" And then, I can see Jesus saying, "All right." "What did You say?" "Yes, ma'am."

Parents are called by God to lead their children in the way they should go—whether the children like it or not.

Key #5: *Teach Appreciation and Contentment*

She said:

Madeline McElveen, whose daughter, Bonnie McElveen, was appointed president of the Red Cross in 2004. Her mother, now in her nineties, emphasized that the family had always gone to church together, and that she'd taught her children that no matter what they were facing, God would help them. Some other notable comments from this woman were, "What you put into your children will always come back out, somewhere along the line." If you raise them in love, it's going to return. She also said, "We were a low-income family, but we lived like we were rich, because we were rich in every area of our lives except for finances." She said that despite their financial struggles, they never felt stressed but rather trusted in God to turn their situation around. When times were tough, the family would gather together and say, "Yes, we're on a journey here, with a few things to work out. But God will bring what we need in due season. In the meantime, let's pray together."

Quite honestly, that's how Larry and I always were with our kids. There were times when we had next to nothing, but the kids never knew we were lacking. We did most of our shopping at Goodwill and garage sales, and our kids were fifteen or older before they ever received a brand-new bicycle. Through those years of having very little and living on a strict budget, our kids thought we were rich. And they thought this because we'd tell them we were! We'd say, "You know what, guys? We are rich. We are so blessed." And they believed us. Just like Bonnie McElveen's family, we were rich in every area except for our finances.

We are thankful that, at this point in our lives, we are financially blessed, more so than ever before. But we still make a point to maintain a sense of appreciation, as well as to practice faithful stewardship.

Teaching our kids to be grateful and appreciative is especially important in today's society of extravagance and immediate gratification. There are so many "in-demand" products that are disposable or become quickly outdated, and it's alarming how many kids in today's culture have little to no regard for how hard their parents work to keep them clothed, fed, and well cared for.

I remember being alarmed once while shopping with Katie, a teenager at the time, for some new school clothes. As we sorted through the racks of jeans, I overheard another young teenage girl screaming at her mom that she wouldn't be caught dead in a pair of cheap jeans. She insisted that she could wear clothes only if they were made by a certain high-end designer. It was all I could do to restrain myself from stepping in and saying something! (I didn't, much to Katie's relief.) Unfortunately, this attitude of entitlement is prevalent among kids today. It is rare to see young people with a genuine appreciation for the sacrifices and hard work of their parents and other family members for their sake. As parents, we must work to cultivate an attitude of appreciation in our children.

Key #6: Monitor Outside Influences

From preschool through college, our kids are our responsibility. We can't just sit back and hope for the best while they go off with a group of kids we don't know to a destination we don't know of to do things we don't know about. Almost every mom featured in *Mother Nurture* said she monitored their children's friends and influences. Even those who were not professing Christians were selective about their kids' associates. And, if she didn't approve of the friends, she said, "Bring him to our house, where I can watch and decide whether he is the type of person I want you hanging around."

THE INFLUENCE OF CLASSMATES AND FRIENDS

Larry and I kept our kids in the public school system; we never enrolled them in a private Christian school. We always told them, "You can hang out with these kids if you are influencing them, but the moment I see that they're influencing you, it's over. You need to influence them. You need to be a light shining into their lives. You need to be the ones who are set apart, who live by a different set of standards." "But everybody else is doing it," they would sometimes protest. Our response was always: "But in this house, we are not going to do it. In this house, this is how we do other things." And then we showed them a different way.

We need to let our children know that they may have to make sacrifices along the way—give up certain friends, separate themselves from certain influences—and that they might feel lonely for a while. But loneliness lasts for only a season, and then God brings new friends into their lives. As a parent, I know it's never easy to see your children lonesome. Yet it is far worse to see them go down the wrong path and end up in destruction because we allowed them to compromise in matters of the soul.

Another thing that Larry and I told our own children from day one was, "We did not raise a thoroughbred to hook up with a donkey. So, it's imperative that you marry a like-minded person who is going in the same direction as our family." Our daughter Anna and her husband, Brandin, were raised in the same youth group at our church, as were our son, Luke, and his wife, Jen. Both couples were best friends long before they started dating and serving God together. When Brandin came to Larry to ask for his daughter's hand in marriage, Larry said, "Listen, Brandin. Anna is my daughter. I have raised her; I have prayed over her from the time when she was in the womb. My kids are my life—my soul. Now,

Anna has fallen in love with you, but there is a path to success that we have planned out for our children, as well as a call from God on their individual lives. If you marry my child, you also marry my family and our calling. When you marry into this family, you bring together your success and hers. And Tiz and I will parent and pastor you both."

This same pattern was in place when Luke married Jen, and it will be in place for Katie and her future spouse. We have been incredibly blessed by God to have such unity, friendship, and harmony in our family, but we have also been very intentional about keeping it that way!

THE INFLUENCE OF FASHION AND CULTURE

In the media lately, there has been a lot of talk about whether schools have the right to monitor and enforce dress codes. On one report I was watching, the discussion centered around the fashion trends of teenage girls. One commentator stated that, as the father of two teenage daughters, he felt it should be up to the parents, not the school, to determine what is "appropriate dress" for their children.

Then, a female commentators spoke up and said, "If the parents would monitor the dress of their daughters, then the schools wouldn't have to! Apparently, the parents are allowing their daughters to leave the house dressed this way!"

Our policy has always been to tell our kids, "We represent the Lord. And we can still be trendy, contemporary, fashionable, stylish, or whatever you want to call it. We can look good without dressing scantily, suggestively, or seductively."

I monitored my daughters' dress until they were old enough to monitor it for themselves. Every so often, as styles changed, we would have a frank chat about current fashion trends and talk about what is and isn't appropriate.

The point is, as Christians, we are called to a higher standard. We are set apart. And that's the truth we need to impart to our kids as we uphold those standards in every area of life.

THE INFLUENCE OF MORAL LAXITY

As parents, it is our responsibility to watch and monitor the direction our kids are taking. Of course, we can't watch over their every move, but we can keep an eye on the overall pulse of their emotional behaviors and patterns. As we pray for them daily, the Lord will give us wisdom, sensitivity, and guidance. Many a mama's prayers have warded off an attack of the enemy! If we, as parents, don't take the responsibility for our children's physical, emotional, and spiritual health, then who will?

The goal is to create a moral compass within your children's hearts that will lead them to make right decisions on their own. Along with the "do's" and "don'ts," we need to give them the "whys," as well, to promote a deeper understanding that will guide them in the truth. It isn't mere behavior modification; it's character molding. There is an old saying that goes, "Yours is not to reason why. Yours is but to do or die." While that may hold true at times, our ultimate goal should be to teach our children the reason "why." As Christians, we know that certain behaviors have to be changed. The miracle is that we are changed from the inside out! When we experience a genuine encounter with the Lord, we receive a whole new set of "want to's"! And this is the same type of morphing that God wants to do within the hearts of our children.

You Can Raise Children of Greatness

He said:

No one really knows how to be a parent before becoming one. Parenting is a path that's full of difficulties, from the time our first child is born until the day our youngest child leaves the nest. And it doesn't end there! By the time we become grandparents, we're experts, right? One of my favorite authors, Mark Twain, is credited with saying, "When I was a boy of fourteen, my father was so ignorant I could hardly stand to have the old man around. But when I got to be twenty-one, I was astonished by how much he'd learned in seven years."

Raising children is a process that never gets easier, because we're always learning. With every phase comes a new set of parenting "rules" to figure out. We may think that the "terrible twos" are the worst...and then our kids become teenagers and we learn the truth. Adolescence is basically a training camp for adulthood—the time when our sons and daughters prepare to become men and women—and it puts a lot of pressure on them.

When my son, Luke, had had his driver's license for a year or so, if he was riding with me in the car, he would say, "Dad, watch out for that car," and "Dad, slow down here." One year prior, I had been the one giving him similar warnings. The shift was part of the process preparing him to leave the nest.

Even if your children are young right now, before you know it, they'll spread their wings and fly away. That's normal. That's how it's meant to be. And we don't have to worry about them if we've brought them up in the *training and admonition of the Lord* (Ephesians 6:4).

She said:

Some months back, my niece said to me, "I really like the way you parent and handle your relationships. Were you always that way?" I had to tell her that, honestly, in the early years, Larry and I were nowhere near as good of parents as we are today. We were busy "changing the world." We were all over the place. But, over the years, the Lord showed us how to be better parents, better grandparents, and better people overall. And isn't that the journey on which we all find ourselves? The past doesn't matter, as long as we learn from it and allow God to use it as a launching pad to propel us toward becoming the people He desires us to be.

Please don't think that Larry and I are claiming to be "superparents." Just know that we believe God will transform your family as He did ours! God has made many wonderful promises concerning our children. (See, for example, 1 Peter 2:9.) Our children are called to show the world the excellence of God. He has the greatest of destinies in store for them. Let's view our children as men and women of God, for that's what we want them to be someday. Pray that God would raise them up to be adults who love and serve Him with their whole hearts.

Points to Ponder and Apply

- Instill values into your children early and often.
- As parents, we need to learn how to communicate with our children—specifically, a unique way to connect with each one of them.
- Our children will hear our "voices"—the wisdom we impart—in their heads for life. What will they be hearing? What bits of advice will they recall? Let's be intentional about the words we use to and around our children.
- It's never too late to help our kids to change for the better.
- Listen to your children's dreams and search for ways to help them explore and enhance their gifts and talents.

◆ Good parenting requires that the parents grow up first. Let's mature into the parents God has called us to be.

◆ Don't be afraid to lay down the law and say, "In this house, we do it this way, because it works better."

Chapter 8

GODLY DISCIPLINE

You know your children are growing up when they stop asking you where they came from and refuse to tell you where they're going.
—P. J. O'Rourke

He said:

We are told, *"Train up a child in the way he should go, and when he is old he will not depart from it"* (Proverbs 22:6). The word choice is interesting. It doesn't say "Raise up a child" but *"Train up a child."* In Hebrew, the word for *"train up"* means "to make the way narrow and conflict its flow." Basically, we are supposed to establish boundaries for our children. If you think about it, God does the same thing with us, but it isn't to constrain us; it's for our benefit. Jesus said, *"Narrow is the gate and difficult is the way which leads to life, and there are few who find it"* (Matthew 7:14; see also Luke 13:24). When we enter through the narrow gate, we live in obedience to God, and He multiplies His blessings back to us.

When it comes to "constricting the flow" in the lives of our children, our choice tactics should be instruction, motivation, and discipline. Instruction lays out our expectations and lets our kids know what we expect of them, as well as what God expects of them. Motivation involves rewarding our kids for doing the right thing. Discipline gets a bad rap, but it's really a good thing, because it shows our kids that we love them, just as God's chastening proves His love for us.

You have forgotten the exhortation which speaks to you as sons: "My son, do not despise the chastening of the LORD, nor be discouraged when you are rebuked by Him; for whom the LORD loves He chastens, and scourges every son whom He receives." If you endure chastening, God deals with you as with sons; for what son is there whom a father does not chasten? But if you are without chastening, of which all have become partakers, then you are illegitimate and not sons. Furthermore, we have had human fathers who corrected us, and we paid them respect. Shall we not much more readily be in subjection

147

to the Father of spirits and live? For they indeed for a few days chastened us as seemed best to them, but He for our profit, that we may be partakers of His holiness. (Hebrews 12:5–10)

If God chastens His children, whom He loves, then He intends for us to chasten our own children, as well. And if we don't discipline them, someone else will: the school principal, the police, the court system, or worse.

She said:

What we really want to do is create a positive path for our children, because God will use us to transform the world through our homes. A lot of people today would rather be just about anywhere else than at home. They would rather talk to anybody in the world than have to face their teenage son in conversation. There are successful, highly influential CEOs who travel the world striking business deals, yet who cannot—or would rather not—talk to their rebellious teenage daughters.

Take heart, moms and dads! Recent polls have shown that the most important influence in the lives of children is their parents. The children who were surveyed said that the approval of their parents matters more than that of their peers. Still, we need to be tuned in to our children. We need to stay connected with them—for life.

He said:

For the first several weeks at the church Tiz and I pastored in Santa Fe, New Mexico, I would be preaching, and kids would be running up and down the aisles, across the platform, and everywhere else they could. Finally, I had a meeting with the parents, and I said, "Listen, guys—you have got to discipline your children. You can't just let them run everywhere." One of the women said, "But I love my little guy too much." I responded, "It isn't your son you love; it's yourself you love." Few parents want to discipline their kids because they want to be their friends.

Bite the Bullet and Put Your Foot Down

She said:

Our children are our responsibility—precious gifts from God. And our job is to give them back to the Lord as a gift. We don't have to watch while the world grabs ahold of our kids. We have the power to get on top of things and monitor them! And we should never be afraid to say no. We should never back down when we feel wary about the influence their friends are having on them.

Parents, let's refuse to allow peer pressure to back us into a corner! We may not be right every time, but we have the right to try to do the right thing. We will make mistakes—I guarantee it. We all do. It's a process of trial and error. But the future of our children is determined largely by the path we let them take. If they say, "I'm sixteen; you can't tell me what to do," our response should be, "Okay, then. If you're sixteen and such a big shot, go pay your own bills and support yourself. But as long as you are living in this house, and as long as I am buying the food you eat, you will live by my rules."

We have a responsibility to take charge of our children. God has placed us in a place of authority, not that we should adopt an attitude and boss our children around, but so that we can commit to their success. Our home is to be their safe haven, not necessarily their happy haven.

The Bible is our ultimate sourcebook on parenting wisdom. Here are a few Scriptures that have been my mainstay through the years.

Train up a child in the way he should go, and when he is old he will not depart from it. (Proverbs 22:6)

Correct your son, and he will give you rest; yes, he will give delight to your soul. (Proverbs 29:17)

Fathers [and mothers], *do not provoke your children to wrath, but bring them up in the training and admonition of the Lord.* (Ephesians 6:4)

What Paul was saying in that final verse is that there are a lot of methods we might use to correct our kids that will produce harmful effects and foster hostility. But there's also a way to correct them and keep them on the right path, and that way comes from the Lord.

He said:

If you've ever watched *The Little Rascals*, you're probably familiar with the character of Spanky. On one particular episode, he gets into trouble at school, and so his teacher sends him home with a note explaining what he had done. He gives the note to his mom, who says, "When your father gets home, you are going to get it."

Now, I don't know how it is in your family, but at my house, the fear of Dad is the beginning of all wisdom. If Dad isn't around, it's Mom the kids should fear. My point is, they need to understand that when they do something wrong, there's a price to pay. Why? Because we love them. And because they're going to pay the price, if not to their parents, then to their school principal, the police, or their parole officer.

Poor Spanky. Those hours he spent awaiting his dad's return were the longest of his life. His dad comes in and says, "Son, this is going to hurt me more than it hurts you," and Spanky's thinking, *No kidding*. But that's reality. Nobody wants to have to discipline his children. However, if we really love our children, we'll set boundaries they are not permitted to cross, because it's better for them to be disciplined by us than to be disciplined by the court system or something even less forgiving.

When our oldest daughter, Anna, started school, we were missionaries in Australia. She came home from her first day of kindergarten and announced, "My teacher is a Christian." We asked her how she could tell. "Did she pray with you?" we wanted to know. "No," Anna said, "the teacher told us, 'I love you kids enough that, if you're bad, I'm going to spank you.'" She had learned to identify spanking with Christians because her mom and I would spank her and say, "This is for your own good."

She said:

It's critical for our kids to understand that wrong behavior results in consequences and repercussions. For many parents, this is a hard nutrient to give their kids!

Larry and I absolutely hate disciplining. More than anything, we dislike having to be the "bad guy." Just the other day, our grandsons, Asher and Judah, were at our house, and Judah did something he wasn't supposed to. I told him that he wasn't to do that, and then I said, "You're going to have a time-out." Of course, even as I said this, my heart was heavy—I was in worse shape than he! But I moved him off to the side of the room and commenced his time-out.

In the meantime, Asher was playing with the puppy, having a good old time. Actually, he was probably exaggerating his enjoyment, just to rub it in his brother's face. When I finally told Judah that his time-out was over, tears began falling down his face, and he said, "Nana, when I had that time-out, I felt like I was separated from my whole family. I felt so alone and not loved." I took him in my arms, and I said, "Judah, honey, you know what? That's what a time-out is meant to do. It's meant to separate you from everything else. It's not that you were ever separated from our love. Nana and Sabba love you, no matter what you do. But when you do something wrong, there has to be a little bit of a sting, so that you won't want to do that wrong thing again. So that you'll think about it the next time and remember how much you disliked the consequences."

Sometimes, parents, it's especially hard for us to be disciplinarians. No parent likes to be the "bad guy." But we need to enforce discipline in order to discourage bad behavior and reinforce good behavior.

John Wesley told a story about a lady who was running errands with her children, pushing some of them in strollers, with the rest of them trailing after her. A man approached her and said, "My, what a beautiful family. I'd give my life for a family like that." And the woman said, "Dear, that's just what it takes." Let's not sugarcoat the fact that if you're going to build a strong family, it will cost you your life.

Back It Up

He said:

Instruction without discipline is useless. If we merely say to our children, "Don't play in the street," and do nothing when they ignores us, several thousand pounds of steel are probably going to come hurtling along and hit them. If we say, "Don't play in the street" we should expect them to listen to us the first time or pay the consequences. In this case, it's much healthier for our children to be disciplined by us, their parents, than to learn that lesson the hard way—maybe even being disciplined at the cost of their very lives.

Nowadays, it isn't in vogue to talk about disciplining children. Somehow, the notion "All you need is love" has become popular. The idea is that our job, as parents, is primarily to love our children. But, one day, they're going to fly away from the nest and find themselves in the real world, far from the shelter of home and the love of their parents. If all they've known is "love"—laxity of discipline—they're in for a real shock.

I can't wait until my grandchildren are old enough to play T-ball and football and so forth—on a team that keeps score. It's fine for them now, as four-year-olds, to play on a team where "everybody wins," and the object is just to have fun. I love watching those little guys hit the ball and then run to the bathroom on their way to first base. It's hilarious. And the score couldn't matter less to them. But there will come a day when they'll need to learn how to play graciously, whether they're winning or losing. They'll need to learn how to celebrate their victories with a proper perspective and how to accept defeat as only temporary. Life is full of battles, from the ball field to the boardroom to the bedroom.

I was watching a comedian who said that in his school, they'd gotten rid of dodgeball because they didn't want the kids getting hit with anything, especially those big, spongy balls. Life is all about getting hit and then getting up again! We need to teach our kids that they are more than conquerors (see Romans 8:37), no matter what life hits them with.

The Bible tells us to "train up" our children. Read what the prophet Isaiah says:

> *Though the Lord gives you the bread of adversity and the water of affliction, yet your teachers will not be moved into a corner anymore, but your eyes shall see your teachers. Your ears shall hear a word behind you, saying, "This is the way, walk in it," whenever you turn to the right hand or whenever you turn to the left.*　　　　　　　　　　　　　　　　　　(Isaiah 30:20–21)

What a tremendous passage of Scripture. It says, "Yes, there will come times when your children are tempted. There will be instances when they'll protest, saying, 'But all my friends are doing it!' Problems will arise. But, one day, parents and teachers will no longer be shoved into the corner." Remember what Hillary Clinton said about how it takes a village to raise a child? That's true, but we'd better make sure it's a Christian village. Let's refuse to let the world push us into a corner and say, "Here's how you should raise your kids." It's up to us to instruct them, motivate them, and discipline them according to the Word of God. That way, when they finally leave the nest, they will know the way to go and will not depart from it.

She said:

Back in the old days, all you needed to discipline your kids was a switch and a bar of soap. I remember being eleven years old and saying a bad word—who knows where I'd picked it up. And I remember having Ivory soap in my teeth for a week and a half. I practically had bubbles coming out of my mouth every time I talked. But it did the job, because I never said another bad word.

When I was a kid, there were definite consequences for rebelling, and I knew it. Not all children will push the envelope and try to get away with whatever they can. But it's crucial that we back up our rules, because kids are smart. They know how to play us. If we say no with our mouth but fail to discipline them when they defy us, then we've waived our authority and influence in their lives. We must be sure to back up our words with corresponding actions. When our kids disobey, they should be able to count on getting spanked, being given a time-out, or being otherwise punished.

Present a United Front

We've said that the point of marriage is not to compete with each other; it's to complete each other. And we do that only insofar as we are united together. Spouses shouldn't let their children pit them against each other! Mom and Dad need to assume the same stance whenever the kids approach them seeking permission to do something. If we present a consistently united front, our home will be a haven of unity. If Mom says no, Dad should say no, too, and vice versa.

He said:

The number one thing in our marriage and in raising our kids has always been that God comes first. It doesn't matter what I'm feeling, what Tiz is feeling, or what the kids want to do—the first question we ask is, "What does the Word of God say on the matter?" You can read all kinds of books on marriage. And you can read the statistics that say divorce is just as common in the church as it is in secular society. But it doesn't have to happen if everybody does his or her part. Both spouses are responsible for making the marriage work and for holding it together.

> *If we present a consistently united front, our home will be a haven of unity. If Mom says no, Dad should say no, too, and vice versa.*

In our home, there was never a power struggle. It wasn't as if we didn't have different views on various issues, but we learned that doing marriage God's way brings blessings, while doing marriage our way, or the way that felt natural to us, brings chaos.

Set Healthy Boundaries

She said:

Whether they know it or not, our kids want boundaries. Psychologists have performed studies based on students at recess, comparing students playing on a playground without fences versus a playground bounded by a fence. The studies showed that at schools with a fence, the students spread out and played everywhere. They spread out to the farthest corners—ball, jacks, you name it. But at the schools where there wasn't a fence, all of the students clustered in the middle of the playground and never strayed to the edge. The truth is, there's safety in fences. Boundaries provide a sense of security.

Some people protest and say, "But I'm going to make an enemy of my kids if I tell them no." I like to remind them of this truth: God didn't call you to be their friend! We are their friends, of course, and we should be. But that isn't our primary role in their lives. Larry and I have always told our kids, "We want to be your friends, but we have to be you parents." We tell the people in our congregation, "We want to be your friends, but we've been called by God to be your pastors." Sometimes, those two roles don't jive. But, in the end, it computes out to create love. Yes, it is possible to go overboard with boundaries. In general, though, boundaries tell our kids that we love them enough to want them to stay on the right path.

He said:

Look now at Romans 12:2: *"Do not be conformed to this world, but be transformed by the renewing of your mind, that you may prove what is that good and acceptable and perfect will of God."* It's up to us, in large part, to set boundaries that will keep our kids from conforming to the world. It's tragic to see parents fueling their children's desire to be like the "role models" they see on MTV—buying their daughters outfits that look like something their favorite pop star would wear and so forth. I don't care how the world dresses. Our children need to be different. They don't need to be dressed like we're living in Elizabethan England, but let's have a little modesty.

When Tiz and I were pastoring in Spokane, Washington, we held a Bible study for teenagers and young adults in our living room. At one of our meetings, we somehow got on the topic of parents, and the common sentiment was, "Pastor, we don't like it when our parents tell us we have to be home at such-and-such time; we don't like it when they tell us we can't do such-and-such." After a while, one young woman spoke up and immediately started to cry. She said, "Most of you don't know, but I have been a prostitute since I was thirteen years old. My parents never told me when I had to come home. My parents never told me who I could and couldn't hang out with. My parents never told me I couldn't smoke dope—they smoked dope in front of me. They didn't care what I did because they were so busy doing their own thing. They didn't care enough about me to say no, and so, right under their noses, I slipped into the world and began to do exactly what I saw them doing." She looked at the other kids and said, "I wish I had parents like yours—parents who loved me enough to tell me no."

No "Dissing" Allowed

She said:

When a baby is born, he's completely selfish. He isn't offering to help with the dishes, to take out the garbage, or to change his own diaper. It's all "Me, me, me." He cries to be fed, changed, held, whatever. So, one of our jobs as parents is to help our children transition out of this phase of complete self-centeredness to a level where they help out rather than insist on being the center of

She looked at the other kids and said, "I wish I had parents like yours— parents who loved me enough to tell me no."

their own universe. This must happen in the family arena. We teach them to be polite and courteous, as well as to respect other people, both their peers and their elders.

One thing Larry and I have never tolerated from our children is disrespect, whether of adults or each other. The other night, Anna and I were shopping, and we saw a mom and her teenage daughter in a store, looking at a $200 pair of shoes. The mom said something like, "Honey, what do you think about these?" You should have seen the look her daughter was giving her—one that screamed disdain. Later, Anna told me, "Mom, it was all I could do not to get in that girl's face and say, 'Your mother is paying two hundred dollars for a pair of shoes for you, and you're making her feel like a loser.'"

The truth is, this attitude is becoming more and more common among kids today. We can't allow it in our households! Our children should not be able to get away with being disrespectful. There have been times at church when I've seen a child treating his or her parents with this disdainful, condescending attitude. When this occurs, I march right up and say, "Excuse me? That's your mother." And then, I turn to the mother and say, "You really let him/her talk to you that way? What kind of a kid are you raising? If he/she disrespects you, he/she will disrespect everybody. It's your responsibility, as the parent, to teach him/her respect."

Larry will tell you that if children are permitted to give "lip"—if they challenge authority without suffering any consequences—then they'll challenge their teachers' authority, they'll challenge the authority of law enforcement officers, and they'll challenge the authority of God. Respect needs to be taught in the home.

For the most part, our kids abided by the rules and met the expectations Larry and I had set for them. There were never any major disciplinary actions required on our part. But the biggest area where adjustments were necessary was in their attitudes. More spankings and time-outs occurred in our household for a bad attitude than for anything else. But their attitudes were under constant assault by the influences of the world.

Respect of their elders is one of the most important things kids can learn, in my opinion. Larry is a big advocate of "Yes, ma'am" and "No, ma'am." I wasn't brought up to use those phrases, but I was taught to respect adults. There's a disturbing trend right now among young people to be cynical and sarcastic. And it isn't acceptable. Nor does it need to be! Kids today treat adults with such disdain and contempt, rolling their eyes, shrugging their shoulders, refusing to look their parents in the eye, and dismissively muttering, "Whatever."

When our children were young, we never let them get away with disrespectful behavior, toward adults or toward each other. We had zero tolerance for condescension. All we have to do is tell our kids, "In this household, we're turning things around. We respect others." If this is an area in which your children struggle, I highly recommend the book *Have a New Kid by Friday.* In it, author Kevin Leman contends that parents have the tendency to put up with disrespect and disobedience on the part of their children. One example he gives is the following: Let's say you're driving your child home from preschool, and she sasses you. If the normal routine is for her to have cookies and milk when she gets home, she doesn't get any today. When she asks, "Mommy, where's my cookies and milk?" you say, "You were disrespectful of me, so no cookies and milk for you today." She may fuss and throw a fit, but you must not give in. There must be repercussions for bad behavior.

Another example: let's say your daughter is now sixteen years old, and she's been sassing you all day. Then, at five o'clock on Saturday night, she wants a ride to a school function. You say, "No, not tonight." "What? Why not?" "Because you sassed me today, and there are consequences." She'll get the point, won't she?

We need to be the adults—the ones who set boundaries, establish consequences, and follow through with them. We need to say, "If you're going to do the crime, you're doing to do the time." It takes commitment and effort on the parents' part. Too often, as parents, we feel that we just don't have the energy to deal with it, so we let it go. But our children's bad attitudes do not just fizzle away; they grow and multiply, almost like a contagious disease. How many times have we found ourselves saying, "If you do that one more time..."? but never follow through with the consequences? It gets to the point where our kids simply tune us out because they know from experience that we're making empty threats.

We're always training our kids, either to listen and obey or to ignore and disobey. I have been guilty of the latter, on occasion. Every so often, I would have to sit down with my children and review the household rules. I would say something like, "I know I've been slack, but from here on out, there are new rules. We are tightening things up. If you do such and such, here's what you can expect as punishment. Understand?" Then, I had to enforce it—or, as Larry would say, "Back it up!"

If our kids don't respect us, they'll never respect anybody else.

It's important to set reasonable consequences that are feasible for us to enforce. We shouldn't tell our kids, for example, that they're grounded for the next fifteen years—yeah, right! That's impossible. But we can enforce smaller, yet no less severe, consequences, such as taking away their cell phones for a week, forbidding them to use the computer for one weekend, banning them from television use for a week, and so forth. Whatever consequences we set, we need to make sure we back them up, because that's the only way we'll get the respect we demand.

He said:

It's crucial that we teach our kids respect. My kids are all in the ministry. They're pastors. Because they were raised up right, they still say, "Pastor Scott," "Pastor Ed," and so forth, even to address their colleagues in ministry. They learned respect.

If our kids don't respect us, they'll never respect anybody else. They learn to respect authority when Mom and Dad command them to. Training up our children is a tough job, but it's worth it. Better they learn respect from us than from the prison system.

Discipline Immediately and Consistently

She said:

When our kids act up, we should deal with it then. If we ignore it, they'll keep it up. Sure, there are times when I feel too tired to deal with an issue. I just want to say, "Whatever" and let it go. But I owe it to my children to deal with their issues, for their ultimate benefit. Sometimes, it's tempting to gloss over things and to say, "No big deal." But it is a big deal. If we deal with a problem the first time, we decrease the likelihood of its happening again.

One afternoon when we were living in Australia, I took three-year-old Luke along with me to run some errands. We had stopped for gas, and I took him inside with me to pay. When we walked back outside, he seemed to be concealing something in his pocket. I asked him, "What have you got there?" "Nothing." "Luke. What have you got there?" "Nothing." "What is that?" He finally showed me what he'd taken—a small piece of a broken toy that he'd found beneath the checkout counter. It probably would have been swept up and trashed, but it was store merchandise, just the same, and he had stolen it. So, I marched him right back inside and made him tell the cashier that he'd stolen the toy. The man said, "Oh, that's nothing; he can have it." But I said, "No, because stealing is stealing. In his mind, he was stealing, and he needs to suffer the consequences for doing wrong." The man insisted, "It's okay, really." But I said, "Nope. He did wrong, and he needs to repent in his heart to make this right." And he did just that.

Back in the car again, I started crying—it isn't easy to force your kids to make amends! But it had to be done. When we returned home, I told Luke that he needed to answer to his dad. And Larry didn't come home for two hours! So, all the while, poor Luke was waiting in the corner, weeping, wailing, and shaking the whole time. And you should have seen me! I was even worse. Believe me, I didn't want to have to do that to him.

Larry finally came home and found out about Luke. After a quick spanking, we took him to his room and said, "You sit there and think about what you did. When you're ready, you can come out."

Larry and I are the same way. We're tough, but we're tender. Finally, Luke came out of his room, and said, "I did wrong. I stole. And I will never do it again." We led him in a prayer of repentance—gave him a soul shower, as I like to call it.

We told him, "Daddy and Mommy love you so much, and we want the best for you. We never want you to travel down a wrong path."

That experience changed his life forevermore. Luke just turned thirty, and he has a consistent moral compass and such integrity of character, both of which have molded him into the strong man and incredible leader he is today. He could have turned out a lot different, had it not been for the lesson he learned at the gas station that day. If I had shrugged it off and said, "Oh, it's a piece of plastic; no need to worry about it," he would have learned that he could pull off theft and get away with it. His heart would have been conditioned not to experience remorse at wrongdoing. This is why we, as parents, must commit to disciplining our children. We have been entrusted with the well-being of the future generation. It's a high calling to shape the world, and a privilege that should not be taken lightly.

That was the first and last time Luke stole. One year later, we had moved back to the States. One day at the grocery store, I was going through the checkout aisle when Luke started saying, "Ma'am? Excuse me, ma'am?" to the clerk. I told him not to interrupt, and he said, "I know, but I found this." It was a $100 bill—big money, he knew. And he was turning it in to the cashier. The point had been made—and the life lesson had been learned—back in that gas station in Australia.

Model Mood Management

When it comes to conflict resolution, we shouldn't let our kids pitch a fit. Yelling, stomping, kicking, and screaming should not be tolerated. Of course, if we parents deal with conflict by pitching fits, screaming, and stomping, we shouldn't be surprised when our kids do the same.

But when we carry ourselves with calmness and act on a higher level of emotional control, we can expect the same kind of behavior from our children. Let's teach them stress management. What happens when there's a problem in the home? Do you panic and freak out, or do you look up and say, "God is going to help us"? Training our kids to keep the faith equips them to react to stressful situations with confidence that their Lord and Savior will carry them through.

Kids can be moody. Some just love to pout! In Australia, they have a special term for someone who pouts and whines: "whinging sook." What does a whinging sook look like? It looks similar to a child whose parent tells her, "You're going to trip on that lip." (That's what my dad always said to me.)

I remember one time, when I was about five years old, something happened on a family camping trip that caused me to get mad at everybody. I sat there and pouted, pouted, pouted. Two hours later, I was still pouting. Meanwhile, the rest of my family was down by the lake, swimming and having fun. While I was sitting there watching them, still pouting, I thought, *I really want to be down there.* But I didn't know how to break out of my funk, you know? Finally, my mom came up to me and said, "Have you had enough pouting? Go on down to the water." She'd allowed me to pout for a while, so that I'd experience my self-made emotional prison, but then she came to free me. I was like, *Thank you! Hallelujah! Someone finally set me free!* And I took off for the lake.

How often we create our own emotional prisons! Pouting and wallowing in self-pity is a dangerous, slippery slope, and we should train our kids not to mope. Whenever my children started moping around the house, I'd say, "That's enough. Snap out of it." In the long run, they were always grateful I did! I have a saying I like to use with my kids, my staff, and even myself: "Excuse me; your attitude is showing!"

We don't want to be pouting all the time, and neither do our kids. They don't want to be held captive by moodiness. So, we need to tell them to get over it and move on, not to wallow in self-pity. Every person is born with an individual emotional makeup and disposition, but each person is also capable of learning new behavior patterns.

Monitor Virtual Networks

We need to pay close attention to the kids with whom our children are hanging out. And we can't afford to forget about the "virtual" friends our kids meet online in chat rooms, on Facebook, on MySpace, and so forth. In our generation, my parents knew who I was hanging out with because they could see them face-to-face. Today, our children have an entire world of friends we don't know—and probably never will.

It may require us to go beyond our technological comfort zones, but we should make sure to monitor our kids' Facebook accounts and MySpace pages. We should ask them to pull up their profiles for a spot check. It's wise not to warn them ahead of time; otherwise, we just give them a chance to delete all traces of anything they don't want us to see.

There are predators out there, targeting our youth; there are "friends" spreading rumors, sometimes with devastating effects. We need to know who our kids are communicating with and who is influencing their lives, because there is a war being waged for their souls. There's a battle being fought over the hearts, minds, and bodies of our children—and, ultimately, their eternal destinies. It's up to us to erect a barrier. We need to create a firewall. Our kids should know that we are watching them, and that anytime we come across a character who doesn't pass muster with us, we're going to ask them why they're talking with this person.

> *There's a battle being fought over the hearts, minds, and bodies of our children—and, ultimately, their eternal destinies. It's up to us to erect a barrier.*

We are not invading their space, believe me. I'll never understand parents who cautiously knock on the locked doors of their kids' rooms and timidly ask, "Honey, may I come in and have a moment?" or parents who allow their kids to lock their doors and plaster them with signs saying "Private! Keep Out!" Come on! Who's paying for that room? Who bought that computer and pays for wireless Internet? Larry and I always respected our kids' privacy and personal space, but not to such a degree that we were oblivious to their activities and friendships. We always kept an eye on our kids and the people they were spending time with.

This isn't just for parents of teenagers. Even when my kids were little, if I didn't like the way their friends were behaving, I no longer permitted them to play together. Starting with their very first playdate, I monitored the children they hung out with. We can't afford to compromise our standards. Instead, we should expect our children to grow and mature continually. Sometimes, we expect more from toddlers than we do from teenagers. Our grandsons, Judah and Asher, learn something new every day. But, sometimes, we enter into this zone where we don't expect any growth from our kids. We need to keep them on a path that's linear and ever improving.

It's also important to make sure our kids have friends who are "real," not only in the sense of being true and loyal, but also being nearby—friends they can get together with and be encouraged by on a regular basis. We live in a real world! I am all for e-mail, Facebook, and other social networks, but it's necessary to have some real interaction with real people.

I know a family of "techies" whose son started seeing a girl. When she went off to college, the two kept up their relationship over the Internet, talking on their Webcams. However, the son didn't limit their conversations to his room. When he and his family would go out to dinner, he would bring his laptop along and set it up in a seat, so that his girlfriend could join them, albeit virtually. And they would talk during the meal! At one point, one of the younger kids was acting up, and the girlfriend spoke over the Webcam, "Brian, straighten up and obey your mom!" Technology is amazing, don't get me wrong. But we need to have real relationships. And we need to keep our children from being sucked into the vacuum that's void of morals, values, and substance.

He said:

Do your children have cell phones? Call them. "Where are you?" "I'm at the mall." "Great. Take a picture and send it to me." "Oh, there's no reception." "Walk outside." Keep on commanding your children. Even when my youngest, Katie, finally moved out of the house, I didn't stop calling her to ask her, "What are you doing? How are you?" She may be twenty-five, but she'll always be my baby.

It's up to us to command our children. It's up to us to ask the tough questions—"Who are you with?"—and to enforce the tough rules—"You're not going with those kids." "But, Mom!" they may protest. "But nothing. You're staying home." As parents, we have the prerogative to impose curfews and manage wardrobes. To those who are afraid of their kids getting mad at them, I say, better that than their getting arrested or getting pregnant.

Maybe Tiz and I were overly strict. After all, we didn't allow our kids to date until they were eighteen. And before our kids dated anyone, they came to us for a consultation, of sorts. I remember Luke coming to me and asking, "What do you think of Jen?" Today, Jen is our children's pastor. Luke met her while they were volunteering at an after-school program for at-risk kids at our church. They didn't meet at a disco; they didn't meet at the mall; they met at church—and in the midst of serving, not just sitting there.

You're probably familiar with the acronym "PK," which stands for "preacher's kid" or "pastor's kid." The label usually has a negative connotation, because preachers' kids are often some of the worst. But Tiz and I decided that it would not be that way in our family. We decided that our kids would not be the worst; they would be the best. And we took it upon ourselves to train them up in the way they should go. We made sure the people we allowed in our home were honorable, God-fearing individuals who would treat our children with kindness and love. We didn't discuss church business in front of them. Tiz never said, "We can't afford that"; she always said, "Let's pray and see what God does." She kept a prayer journal, and we would talk with our children about the miracles God had done for our family and for other people in our church family.

We were purposeful in our conversations and always promoted a positive atmosphere of compassion toward others and gratefulness toward God for what we had. What we cultivated in our children at a young age, they have kept up until now: they are God-centered, family-oriented adults who are genuinely compassionate about helping people. As Tiz has said, we teach what we know, but we reproduce what we are. Remember, God will help you on this exciting journey of building a wonderful family!

Give "Showers" of Love

She said:

After we've disciplined our children, we need to shower them with love and encouragement, so that they will come to view repentance as a positive thing. Repentance is an act of turning the other way and not going back. It's a process we need to model for our children by showing them how to come before the Lord and say, "God, I am sorry for how I've behaved. Please cleanse my heart and help me to resist further temptations to do the same thing." After that, we show them love by restoring them—reminding them how much we love them, in spite of their wrongdoing; telling them that our desire is to keep them on the right path and that the only way to do that is through correction. It's important to affirm that they themselves are not bad, just their behavior, so they'll understand that our love for them is unconditional.

A potted plant needs to be pruned every now and then; cutting off the dead blossoms makes way for new growth. Otherwise, those "deadheads" suck all of the life out of the plant, robbing it of the nutrients it needs to thrive. In the same way, we need to remove the bad parts from the lives of our children in order that they may produce good fruit. We edit those negative things, so to speak, and then we extend forgiveness, welcoming them back with open arms, because we forgive them as an illustration of how God has forgiven all of us.

Now, when we commit to lift up our children, to affirm them, and to accentuate the positive while eliminating the negative, we still have to deal with whatever issues they may be facing. We still need to be involved in their lives, not to the point where we stifle them, but enough that we become aware of any red flags indicating trouble. God will grant us wisdom, if we'll only trust Him and pray daily for our family, covering our spouse and children with the protective blood of Jesus. We should always pray that they would be clothed in the armor of God, so that the ways of the world will not infiltrate and influence them. And we should spend time with them.

Sometimes, there are deep-seated issues, and we wonder how to deal with them. A parent whose child has gone astray or a spouse with serious problems in marriage often experience a desire for retribution—a desire for that wayward child or hurtful spouse to pay the price. But loving someone unconditionally is not the same as condoning his or her behavior. It just means loving someone despite all of his or her flaws.

> *Loving someone unconditionally is not the same as condoning his or her behavior. It just means loving someone despite all of his or her flaws.*

A dear friend of mine was raised in a Christian home by parents with extremely strict standards. Yet, despite all of the family rules and regulations, my friend went astray. Early in her teenage years, she got involved with the wrong crowd. Her mother tried to keep her on the straight and narrow, but she went her own way and ended up getting caught stealing. Even after she and her friends had spent time in jail for their crime, they did it again. She couldn't resist the peer pressure. Her streak of rebellion became stronger, and she defied her parents and God.

When this young woman ended up back in jail, her mom admitted that she didn't know what to do with her daughter. She cried out to God, saying, "What do I do to bring her back?" Then, her mom—this prim and proper little Christian lady—drove to the prison to see her daughter, who had been there three years and had four years left of her sentence. This petite, meek woman met with her daughter and told her what she felt the Lord was telling her to say. Instead of telling her daughter how ashamed she was of her, she pressed her palms against the glass separating them and said, "Honey, I am so glad to see you. I've missed you so much, and I love you so much. I'm so proud of you."

At that moment, my friend collapsed in tears. She later told me she hadn't cried for fifteen years. And it was because the love of her mother had pierced through her hardened layers and won back her daughter to the love of the Father. That love transcended all of the hardness her soul had been encased with. And she sobbed and said, "Mom, Mom, I need to come back to the Lord." So, her mother prayed for her, right there in the prison, and her daughter received the Lord into her heart. Soon thereafter, her daughter started leading a Bible study for her fellow inmates. When she got out of prison, she came to our church and became a true leader with a heart full of compassion who touched the lives of hundreds of hurting people in our ministry. And it was all because of the power of unconditional love.

Today, some parents are looking at the flowers that are their children and saying, "God, I see some deadheads. My family is starving for Your Spirit." Guess what? God is a restorer. Everything the enemy has taken from us, God has promised not only to restore, but to restore one hundredfold. The King of Kings is ready to meet our needs, above and beyond our greatest expectations. To every family, even the ones who feel less than stellar, God is saying, "I'm going to use your family as an example. I'm going to bring restoration to you so that the world will know what I am capable of." If the enemy hasn't stolen anything significant, you have the opportunity to go from good to great. Let's be that family, that institution, that shows the world how great and loving our God is.

Discipline Is Worth the Effort

Being consistent as disciplinarians can be tough, but it's worth it, especially when we remember that our children's ultimate destiny—the place where they'll spend eternity—depends a lot on how we raise them. Just because you and I call God our Lord and Savior doesn't mean that our children automatically will. There's a saying that goes, "God has no grandchildren, only children." Our children need to experience the Lord firsthand if they're going to find eternal salvation. That's why the example we set is so important.

We've got to start when they're young. My children didn't start serving God when they were twenty. No, they gave their hearts to the Lord as little children, around five or six years old. The Spirit of God moved in each one of them individually, and something ignited inside of them. But in order to get to that point, they had to know about God, to be admonished and corrected according to His ways.

This summer, we were supposed to go on a family vacation. But, due to the fact that our house in Portland was still on the market, as well as some other factors, Larry and I were not prepared to finance a trip. So, we suggested postponing the trip until the house sold. Anna told me that Brandin reacted by saying, "I'm so sad we aren't going to have our family time this summer. I was so looking forward to hanging out with the family." And then, he said, "Tell Mom and Dad that if they need a loan, I'll pay for the family vacation." How about that? The book of Proverbs says that if we raise our families right, our children will rise up and call us blessed. (See Proverbs 31:28.) If we plant the seeds and give them the proper nutrients, we're going to reap a great harvest.

Is every day a walk through the rose garden? No. Every family has challenges and issues to overcome. It's a fact of life. But we have a way to get through them, together. With God as our guide and support, we can rest assured that we'll stay on the path to family success. Whenever we stumble, we can take comfort in knowing that *all things work together for good to those who love God, to those who are the called according to His purpose* (Romans 8:28). God bless you and honor you as you continue on this exciting journey of releasing God's blessings in your family!

Prayer

Father, we come into agreement with You and Your plans for our families. Father, we ask that Your Word, Your promises, and Your commandments would become the voice in our heads, as well as in our children's heads. Father, we ask that You would rise up strong among us. Become the voice that leads us and guides us as our moral compass, Lord.

Father, we come into agreement as we break every generational curse that has tried to annihilate the family as You intended it to be. God, we break every curse that would bring division, discord, and disruption into our homes, and we break the secular spirit that tries to destroy the dignity of monogamous marriage and strong families. We break every curse over the young people in our families that would try to draw them into sin and drag them into the world. We break every generational curse that might drive those young people into sin, and we plead the blood of Jesus Christ over them right now.

Now, Father, we ask You to reverse every curse and to release generational blessings. Let us stand in the gap for righteousness. Let us be set apart as examples of Your goodness, Your patterns, and Your love.

Father, let us raise up a generation who hears your voice and spreads Your Word throughout the world. Let us stand out, a testimony to the hope of the world, which is You, Lord. And, Father, let us be an example of what You can do in us, for us, and through us. Lord, I pray for those who are feeling discouraged or dealing with past regrets. We know that with You, there is no condemnation. There is only Your love and Your grace moving us toward a new life and a new beginning. Bring restoration, God. Bring wholeness.

Lord, we claim Romans 8:28: *"All things work together for good to those who love God, to those who are the called according to His purpose."* If we have failed, let us "fail forward." You are a restorer who gives us hope of things to come. We thank You, Lord, for our children. Raise them up as a generation after Your heart, and let them be strong in the land. Send our children into the schools, Lord, and let them be Your voice and an example of Your goodness, strength, and love. Equip them and anoint them, God, to live for You. Smear them with Your abilities and raise them up in the land, God, to glorify You all of their days! Amen.

Points to Ponder and Apply

+ Establish clearly defined expectations for your children and be sure to communicate them often.

+ Use positive reinforcement as much as possible to motivate your children.

+ Make discipline an act of love and fairness.

+ Don't make empty threats. If you set a rule and establish a consequence for breaking it, you should follow through.

+ You and your spouse should be a united team. Don't allow your children to pit you against each other, for a house divided will fall. (See Mark 3:25.)

+ When your children ask permission to do something, go with them to God's Word to see what He says about it.

+ Keep your children's attitudes in check. Remember, "No 'dissing' allowed!"

+ When issues arise, don't put off dealing with them, of you'll lose an important opportunity to correct your children's course.

+ Stay up-to-date with the latest technology, especially as it concerns social networking, so that you can keep an eye on all of your children's friends, "real" and virtual alike.

+ If you consistently shower your children with love and encouragement, they will always come back for more.

PART III:

Release Blessings on Your Home

Chapter 9
MAKING YOUR HOME A HAVEN

Home is the place we love best and grumble the most.
—Billy Sunday

She said:

According to a survey I read, 94 percent of Americans identified "home" as the most important place in the world. Yet the majority of those respondents said, in effect, "We want our home life to be great, but we aren't sure how to get it there." Countless people are trying to figure out how to build good marriages, how to merge successfully into blended families, how to raise good children who are on a positive course in life, and so forth.

I didn't grow up in a family of practicing Christians. We attended church on Christmas and Easter, but we didn't really know the Lord, even though we lived by a moral code that basically modeled Christian ethics. So, throughout my growing-up years, it was this code of ethics, as well as the special bond of love I had with my family, that kept me from straying too far into the world. Because I had a great relationship with my parents, whenever I went out into the world as a teenager and saw the options available to me, my primary thought was how much hurt and shame it would cause them if I were to participate in those things.

Both of my parents worked, so my siblings and I were basically latchkey kids from first grade on. But they made it work. We had dinner together as a family almost every night, with plenty of laughter and conversation around the table. If Mom or Dad had to work late, we would pack a sack dinner and take it to their office so that we would still have a meal together. No matter what, my parents made sure that we knew how much they loved us. They made sure we realized that they were in our corner. I'm not saying that I stayed completely out of trouble or resisted every temptation, but, for the most part, when the world dangled its temptations in front of me, I would say to myself, *Why would I give up what I have at home for what's out there?* I never considered selling out my family in exchange for whatever the world had to offer.

If a happy, peaceful home environment is able to be achieved by families who don't profess to follow God, how much more so should those of us who know Him as Savior and Lord experience His blessings in our homes? If we hope to protect our kids from the world and its allure, we need to make our homes better than it is out there.

This has always been a goal of Larry's and mine, and, by the power of God, the strength of our family relationships, as well as their godly upbringing, has deterred our children from multiple paths that promised nothing but adversity.

Reality Check

Yet, in the average home today, there is far more chaos and confusion than there was in the typical household of any of the generations before us. Our kids are confused. They're searching for fulfillment and happiness, but they aren't even warm. And the reason is that parents are not bringing their children to church or raising them *"in the admonition of the Lord"* (Ephesians 6:4). As a result, these children, all of them searching for a way to fill the void in their hearts, are left vulnerable to the influences of the secular media and other ungodly things. Even students in elementary school are faced with the pressure to do drugs and participate in immoral activities that most of the members of our generation didn't encounter until high school, at the earliest.

Every day, young people are bombarded with peer pressure to live a certain way, to look a certain way. It's impossible to turn on the television without hearing the latest celebrity gossip. Most of us take one look at the tabloids and think, *Who cares?* But the influence on our children is real, and it's loosening their morals and making them shallow. They become caught up in celebrity gossip and Hollywood drama, to the point where their primary concerns are what their favorite stars are doing and how they're dressing. Let's create a life with some substance! There was once a day when you didn't have to force your kids to go outside to play. You never had to convince them to spend time with other kids. Today, however, they're content to sit holed up in their rooms with their laptops, carrying on relationships via the Internet.

The world is full of people in rehab, counseling, and therapy, all of them seeking treatment for their symptoms. I don't want to treat the symptoms; I want to cure the cause. I want to get to the heart of what is causing these symptoms.

Many people are in therapy as a result of growing up amid broken family relationships. And we understand that. Some of us even face those kinds of issues today. It's time to make some corrections. We need to recognize what has gone wrong, and our hand in it, and turn it around. Larry and I have had to do this many times. There would be occasions when we could realize, *Man, it's been months since our family has done anything together.*

This is one of the reasons we started observing *Shabbat* together—to set aside a regular time to come together as a family and rebuild our relationships instead of allowing them to slip away and disintegrate. All week, we're doing all sorts of things, running in a million different directions, but on Friday night at sundown, we come together, light the candles on the menorah, and reconnect with each other. We sit down and have dinner together without the television blasting in the background; it isn't every man for himself, eating dinner in separate rooms or while traveling by car from one activity to the next. Through *Shabbat*, we draw strength from God connecting His "super" to our "natural," as well as simply from being together with our families.

The Influence of Home

Home is where we construct the foundation on which our entire lives are built. It's the heart of everything we will become. Our emotions, our sense of self-esteem, our confidence, our values, our traditions, our morals, our faith, our social skills—every aspect of our identity is birthed out of our family experience, right there in the home. It's where we laugh till we cry and cry till we laugh.

Home is where we learn to forgive, as well as how to accept forgiveness. It's where we learn our people skills that we'll take into our adult lives. Family creates the backdrop of our dreams and gives us the backbone to fulfill them. Home and family ought to be the wind beneath our wings. God has designed them to give us the confidence to go into life and become successful. We should never underestimate the value of social skills! Statistics show that success in business is 20 percent product knowledge and 80 percent people skills. So, it's crucial that we teach our children how to interact with others, starting at a young age.

Creating a Peaceful Home Environment

It's easy to allow chaos and turmoil to take over the home. It's human nature to succumb to strife and grumbling. Again, we have to decide to take the high road. The times we have to spend as a family are precious and rare, so let's do all that we can to keep them positive.

Speak Positive Words

One important key is learning how to talk about good stuff—the things of God—and avoiding negative conversations. Some people seem to gravitate toward negative conversation—they're full of complaining and grumbling. There have been times when a friend has called me and invited me to meet her for lunch and some "girl talk," and I've thought to myself, *No, I'd rather not; it'll cost me too much.* I don't mean from a monetary perspective. *No, because she's toxic. Every word that comes out of her mouth is tainted—not by sin, but by cries and complaints.* It's always "Woe is me."

The other day, I stopped at the grocery store to pick up a few items, and I greeted the man in the produce section. "How are you doing today?" I asked with a smile.

"Well, this weather, I'll tell you. Even though I'm inside, it affects me, you know? I remember a good summer, back ten, twelve, years ago...."

I thought, *I did not sign up for this.* All I wanted was some pleasant chitchat. A little "I'm fine, thank you." But some conversations are simply toxic, no getting around it. They spiral down, down, down, dragging your spirit with them. We've got to bring the level up! We need to create an upward spiral of conversation in our homes, in our families, in our lives. By producing a faith-boosting atmosphere in the home, we create an environment that is compatible with miracles.

> *By producing a faith-boosting atmosphere in the home, we create an environment that is compatible with miracles.*

When Larry and I were young rookie pastors, we'd often ask our mentor for keys in the ministry. One piece of advice, in particular, went straight to our souls. He said, "You will win or lose revival during the car ride home from church." Think about it. If you head home, allowing the Spirit of God to move as you talk about the victories He's won and the lives He's transformed, your life changes. But if you get in the car and immediately start talking about how many people were absent that morning, then you submit to the gravity of human nature, which drags you down.

So, thirty-five years ago, Larry and I made a choice to keep our conversations upbeat on the way home from church. Even if there was only one person in the pew, we refused to dwell on the negative. We determined to speak only about the promises of God. Even if that one person in the pew was asleep for the entire service, we still praise the Lord, trusting that He'll fulfill His promise to let no word return to Him void. (See Isaiah 55:11.)

Let's accentuate the positive and eliminate the negative in every realm of life. When our kids come home from school, let's speak positive words of encouragement and faith rather than rehash all of the negative junk that happened that day.

When our family gets together, we simply don't discuss negative issues or problems. We avoid topics we know will stir up strife. When we come together, we are deliberate about celebrating that time and having fun as a family. A lot of our conversation centers around what the Lord has been doing in our lives and in the world. Also, as a family of avid bookworms, we also like to talk about what we've been reading. There are always fascinating spiritual revelations or current topics to share and discuss.

One time, I heard Anna say to someone, "In our family, we don't like to have normal conversations. We talk about world events. We talk about what's going on in Haiti and other places around the world. There's very little chitchat and small talk. We're either talking about what the Lord is doing around the world or celebrating what He's doing in the lives of people we know, because it validates what we do and also brings us closer together as a family."

I often hear parents complain that they have nothing to talk to their kids about. Here are a few options: talk about Sunday's sermon. Discuss the message. Compare notes on how you've seen God working in the lives of others. Pray together. Sit down to dinner with your children, or over a bucket of chicken or whatever, and ask them, "What did that word mean in your life? How does that apply to you? Did you hear that one testimony about the woman who was in a car accident and went into a coma, but God healed her? Can you believe what God did?"

Let's keep the Word of God alive in our homes and in our families. When we exit through the church doors after a service, let's take revival along with us and allow the blessings of God to descend upon our households.

Whenever I hear that someone was healed of cancer or find out about another wonderful testimony, I want to share it with my children, so that they can rejoice along with me and feel validated in what they're doing.

Avoid Negative Confessions

It's the easiest thing in the world to talk about our problems. The next time you go out for dinner at a restaurant, take a look around at the other couples. It's sad how many of them have nothing to talk about, other than maybe a discussion over whether to order chicken or steak. When Larry and I go out, just the two of us, we're always talking about what God's been doing. We find some common ground and we keep the negative out of our conversations.

It must be a conscious decision to dwell in the positive—in the realm of possibilities—and to discuss such things as our personal visions for our lives and the goals we want to accomplish. Let's refuse to magnify the problems that are going on in the world and magnify the promises of God, instead. None of us wants to be a Debbie Downer who rains on everyone else's parade! Let's speak expectantly about the wonderful things God has in store for our lives. Instead of rehashing our problems with our spouse or children, let's talk about what God can do when we trust in Him.

Embrace Laughter and Fun

Another way that we can create a positive environment and connect with each other is by having fun together. Many parents struggle with this, too, because they feel that their interests and their kids' interests are completely incompatible.

The other day, I saw a family photo taken on a vacation to Monument Valley in Arizona. In the picture, the son was stretched out on a rock, playing with a Game Boy. Although he was physically present with his family, he was not emotionally engaged. How do we bridge this gap?

I counseled a family in which the parents were feeling disconnected from their thirteen-year-old son. They told me that he had been withdrawing further and further into his shell, and that whenever the family got together, he still retreated to the corner to play games on his cell phone. This scenario is far from uncommon today, and, while this type of behavior isn't necessarily a serious issue—sometimes, kids just need a little space—it's important for us as parents to establish certain boundaries; to specify when solitary activities are appropriate and when it's important to join the group.

In our family, we've always tried to find common ground with the kids—a unique way to connect with each of them—on a daily basis. We also scheduled routine family nights.

Usher In the Peace That Passes Understanding

What can we do to create an atmosphere of spiritual maturity in our homes? And I'm not talking about being so heavenly-minded that we're of no earthly value. I'm not talking about spewing Scriptures all day long or being totally disengaged from the natural world.

Here's what I am talking about: when we check the mail, and all we find are bills for the gas, the electric, the mortgage, and everything else, how do we react, and what does that say to our children? Do they see us crumble in a heap on the floor, sick with worry over how we're going to make ends meet? Or, do they hear us say, "We have some challenges to meet. Let's gather round and pray. Let's lay hands on these bills and pray, 'Father God, give us faith in Your miraculous provision'"?

There will be issues that we need to talk about, some of them unpleasant—financial issues, medical decisions, and so forth. We just need to make sure we're discussing the challenges from the standpoint of faith that God will provide a solution. Let's avoid moving in an endless cycle of blaming and complaining. We should find out what the Bible has to say about our particular situation and then choose a scriptural promise to stand on. Larry and I always stand on Romans 8:28: *"And we know that all things work together for good to those who love God, to those who are the called according to His purpose."*

Find out what the Bible has to say about your particular situation and then choose a scriptural promise to stand on.

When the enemy is at the door, we need to make sure our children hear us crying out to God. That way, when the miracle comes in response to our prayers, they'll know that we serve a good and faithful God. In times of trouble and triumph alike, we should gather our children around for family prayers and praise. We must also take advantage of every opportunity to pray with our children. I used to drive my kids to school, and the trip took twenty minutes. So, we would get in the car, and I'd say, "Come on, kids, let's pray." I would lead them first in the Lord's Prayer, followed by a prayer in which I would cover them with the blood of Christ and bind the enemy's power to harm them. When they were a little older, I handed off the baton and let them do the praying. The next thing I knew, my children were praying stronger prayers than I was! This is the blessing that comes when we create an atmosphere of faith and God's presence in our home.

Tammy is a single mom of four teenage children, and her family lost everything in the devastation of Hurricane Katrina. They had nothing left in the wake of the storm. The government moved them to temporary housing here in Dallas. Tammy saw our program on television and said, "Kids, God's going to give us a new beginning. We're going to see Pastor Larry and Tiz, and we're getting our new beginning. We don't have anything, but we're going to gain everything."

Talk about a seemingly hopeless situation! Tammy and her kids were among the thousands who were displaced by the storm and basically dumped in our city. But she decided that they weren't going to be victims—they were going to be victors. The first time she came to church, she introduced herself to me and said, "Pastor Tiz, God's giving me a new beginning. I want to work; I want to be productive. I don't want to be a victim; I want to be a victor. I want to be a good mother to my children, and they want to be good workers and to serve God." We prayed together.

Within two days, she had secured a new job, better than any position she'd held prior to the hurricane. And her starting salary was $10,000 more than she'd been making in her former job. Four years later, all four of Tammy's kids had gotten a steady job and were earning promotion after promotion. Tammy has a van that is fully paid off. God gave her a brand-new home, and when she closed on the house, the seller decided to throw in all new appliances. All of these blessings were the result of Tammy's decision that, no matter what the world threw at her family, they were going to stand on the promises of God. Instead of getting up every morning and saying, "Woe is me! How am I ever going to make it?" she said, "God, what do You have for me today?"

I'm telling you, God will give you a new beginning, just as He did for Tammy and her kids. It doesn't matter where we come from. It doesn't matter what the enemy has stolen from our lives—God has a new life for each of us. He isn't through with us yet. In fact, we've just started down a new path!

You may be in a marriage that's being challenged, as Larry and I were years ago. What God did for us, He's going to do for you. Let's all sit down with our spouses tonight and say, "Today is a turning point in our life as a couple. We aren't going to live in a spirit of contention any longer. We're going to stop wallowing in self-pity. By the power of God, we're going to live in victory and experience His promises in our life and our marriage."

Again, we don't need to pray 24/7 or quote Scripture every time we open our mouths. But we need to create in our homes an environment where the love of God—and our love for God—are evident. Our kids need to see that when challenges come our way, their parents—Mom and Dad, husband and wife—don't complain and grumble but rather call out to God and trust His Word rather than the world. We train up our children through our conversation, through the way we respond to situations, and through the integrity and honesty with which we operate.

We train up our children through our conversation, through the way we respond to situations, and through the integrity and honesty with which we operate.

We can't live according to the maxim "Do as I say, not as I do." Our children will mimic what we do, down to the minutest detail. Children are like little recorders. They play back exactly what we say to them. I'm sure you've lost count of the times your kids or grandkids spoke something you said. They repeat your words because they've absorbed them into their spirits. They become like little clones. I love the saying "We teach what we know, but we reproduce who we are." Nowhere is this truer than in our homes. Our responsibility is great, but it's also a great privilege.

Provide Loving Acceptance and Affirmation

Every single human being craves acceptance. Our children crave it. Our spouses crave it. That's why people go looking for love in all the wrong places—they're seeking affirmation. They're looking for someone to tell them, "You are worth something. You count for something. You are important." This differs from encouragement, because encouragement says, "Honey, you can do it. I believe in you." But affirmation and acceptance says, "I value you. You have intrinsic worth that I recognize."

As parents, we need to be the wind beneath our children's wings. We need to give them the support and structure they long for. Too many kids receive deficient acceptance and affirmation at home, so they end up seeking those things in all the wrong places. If we're going to do one thing right, let's make sure it's pouring loving affirmation into our kids. We can set all the boundaries we want, we can be the strictest disciplinarian on the block, but success in those areas pales in comparison to the ability to affirm and encourage our children. Affirmation creates an atmosphere of love, acceptance, faith, and hope. It has the power to break curses and to release generational blessings.

> If children live with criticism, they learn to condemn.
>
> If children live with hostility, they learn to fight.
>
> If children live with fear, they learn to be apprehensive.
>
> If children live with pity, they learn to feel sorry for themselves.
>
> If children live with ridicule, they learn to feel shy.
>
> If children live with jealousy, they learn to feel envy.
>
> If children live with shame, they learn to feel guilty.
>
> If children live with encouragement, they learn confidence.
>
> If children live with tolerance, they learn patience.
>
> If children live with praise, they learn appreciation.
>
> If children live with acceptance, they learn to love.
>
> If children live with approval, they learn to like themselves.
>
> If children live with recognition, they learn it is good to have a goal.
>
> If children live with sharing, they learn generosity.
>
> If children live with honesty, they learn truthfulness.
>
> If children live with fairness, they learn justice.
>
> If children live with kindness and consideration, they learn respect.
>
> If children live with security, they learn to have faith in themselves and in those about them.
>
> If children live with friendliness, they learn the world is a nice place in which to live.[5]

Teaching children to change the world must start at home.

Be a Blessing, Not a Curse

Our home should be a sanctuary—a place where we're safe from the schemes of Satan. The enemy will try to wreak havoc in the home by assaulting it with spirits of contention, disorder, and division. Let's put our foot down and determine to keep our home a place of refuge.

Let's also determine to be a blessing as we go in and also as we go out. We need to take the light of Christ out into the world, by all means, but let's not extinguish it when we're at home! The home is where we dress ourselves with the

---

[5]Dorothy Law Nolte, "Children Learn What They Live," 1972.

armor of God every morning and say, "No matter what the world is saying, our home is a godly place—a place where faith flows. Our home is a haven of joy."

We should avoid making the home a dumping ground for emotional baggage. I was counseling a married couple in which the wife had children from an earlier marriage. Her husband complained that she let her kids come over and dump all of their emotional baggage on her, and then they'd turn and walk out the door, back to their dad's house, leaving her burdened down. I told the wife not to let them do that. We don't let our neighbors come and dump trash in our yard, do we? No! Neither should we let anyone come and drop his or her baggage in our lap with the expectation that we'll make it magically disappear. Let's declare that our house is a negative-free zone where we stand in victory on the promises of God.

He said:

It's wise to put a mezuzah on as many doors as possible. This comes from the biblical teaching about putting the Word of God on the doorposts of our homes. A mezuzah represents the Word of God and our commitment to following His Word in our homes. (See Deuteronomy 6:6–9.)

We started putting mezuzahs on our doors years ago, when Katie was ten years old. I remember overhearing one of her friends ask her, "What's this on your bedroom door?" Katie replied, "That's a mezuzah." Then, she explained its purpose: "To remind me that I am blessed when I go out and blessed when I come in. It's also to remind me that this blessing works only when I am a blessing when I go out and a blessing when I come in."

One of my friends confessed to feeling that "home" was the one place he could let his hair down, relax, and "let it all hang out." After hearing our teaching on mezuzahs, he finally understood what that little piece of metal hanging on the right-hand side of the door really stood for. He started touching it every time he entered his home, and, as he did, he decided to bring the joy of the Lord into his home and to his family. He said that it really did bring joy to his family and ushered in a peace that had not been in his home for years. God has a plan, and it works!

Let's decide that no matter what happens at school or at work, when we walk into our homes, we'll leave it out in the street. Too many times, the world beats us up, and then we come home and beat one another up. This shouldn't be! No matter what our family is going through, every curse is broken, and every blessing is released, in Jesus' name.

Make Your Home a Happy Place

She said:

Our homes should be happy places. We need to establish an environment that attracts our family members. If our homes are characterized by toxic environments, they will repel our family members. No one wants to live that way. Let's get off of the emotional roller coaster. You may be thinking, *She doesn't know the problems I have at home.* True, I don't know your specific situation. But I have been through my share of hardship, and Larry and I have had to learn how to be more than conquerors. (See Romans 8:37.) We've had to learn to trust. To choose to believe. After thirty-five years of trusting and believing, I can tell you it works! And what God has done for us, He will do for you.

Points to Ponder and Apply

- Try to make your home a haven of love and joy—a place where your children have fun and actually want to spend time.

- Schedule family meals as often as you can—once a week, at the very least.

- When you talk to your children about the things they shouldn't do, make sure to emphasize the blessings of following God's path. Don't make it a negative lecture.

- Keep your smile loud and your voice soft.

- Try observing *Shabbat* every Friday. It is a wonderful provision of God for the family, and it provides incredible blessings.

- Don't gossip, especially in front of your children. Be mindful of your conversation at all times.

- Talk to your children about God's miracles in order to build their faith.

- Don't listen to a "Debbie Downer"—and don't be one yourself!

- Be your children's loudest cheerleader. Praise creates a climate for success.

Chapter 10
RAISING YOUR KIDS FOR CHRIST

*To bring up a child in the way he should go, travel that way
yourself every once in a while.*
—Josh Billings

She said:

A key to creating a peaceful atmosphere in the home, as we mentioned, is the presence of God. It follows that an essential part of our parenting "strategy" should be to cultivate in our children a love for the Lord and a hunger for His Word. Sure, our kids were raised in the ministry—that can be a plus. But it can also backfire and result in children who resent God and His church. Please don't listen to the devil when he whispers, "Easy enough for her to say—her kids grew up in the ministry, so of course they love God." Often, the opposite occurs. PKs, or preachers' kids, have quite the reputation.

Our kids were always on display. I'll never forget one Sunday at our first church, in Santa Fe. Larry was preaching about families, with an emphasis on how to discipline your kids. I was a young mother at the time, and I had three-year-old Anna sitting next to me, coloring. Larry's saying, "Discipline your kids," and "Don't let them be unruly." In the next moment, Anna takes a huge wad of bubble gum out of her mouth and sticks it to the wall. I was horrified! Everyone was looking at me, and I thought, *Oh no, my model child!*

It's Up to Us

As parents, we have an obligation to uphold godly standards in the home. If we allow our children to become lax in this area, abiding by the standards of the world instead of the standards of God, the next thing we know, they're stepping closer and closer to the gates of hell. Compromising won't do them any favors, and it certainly won't promote a heavenly destiny for our children.

Our kids become what we are. Our spouses, in certain ways, will become what we are. If you are a father, it's important that you set an example of trusting

God and serving Him, because, if it's important to you, it'll be important to your wife and children. If you are a mother, the words that you speak are literally being breathed into the mouths of your children. Parents should make sure it's evident to their children that their lives are built on a foundation of God's promises and commandments. They should manifest this not only in what they say but also in what they do—their foundation must prove itself in real-life situations.

He said:

Proverbs 22:6 charges parents to *"train up a child in the way he should go, and when he is old he will not depart from it."* In this verse, the word *"child"* in Hebrew connotes "child of God." Remember, our children aren't really ours; they're on loan to us from God. By having sex that results in a baby, we are telling God that we are responsible enough to raise His child. And if we neglect to raise our children well, ancient Jewish wisdom says that we're committing treason against God and against all that is holy. That's a sobering thought.

God isn't anti-fun, but He is against those things that would rob His children of the wonderful destiny He has in store for them.

Raising up our children does not mean denying them "fun and games." God isn't anti-fun! But He is against those things that would rob His children of the wonderful destiny He has in store for them. Jesus said, "I came to give you life, and life more abundant. (See John 10:10.) But you've got to do it My way."

When we command our children according to the ways of God, we reap incredible blessings. Consider the example of Abraham:

> And the LORD said, "Shall I hide from Abraham what I am doing, since Abraham shall surely become a great and mighty nation, and all the nations of the earth shall be blessed in him? For I have known him, in order that he may command his children and his household after him, that they keep the way of the LORD, to do righteousness and justice, that the LORD may bring to Abraham what He has spoken to him." (Genesis 18:17–19)

Why was Abraham picked by God to be blessed? Because God looked at him and said, "I can see that Abraham is going to command his family and his household—those who work for him—to serve Me. He's not going to abide any sin. He's the type to say, 'If you're in my house, you're going to serve the Lord. If you're working for my business, you're not going to cheat anybody.'" That's what it means to *"do righteousness and justice."* Why will you and I be picked by God to be blessed—to lend, not borrow; to be the head and not the tail? Two things: righteousness and justice.

What people witness behind the pulpit and in the pews should be the same things they witness on the job and in the home. In this day and age, it isn't unusual to hear people say, "We don't really care if the pastor commits adultery." We need to care. We need to hold each other accountable, starting with our children.

"Well," someone might say, "I can't do anything once the kids are out of the house." Fine. But while they're in the house, command them! Tell them, "You live in this house, so you're going to church—with a good attitude. You don't feel like it, you say? Then, I guess you don't feel like eating or watching television, either." If we command our children while they're at home, they'll grow up serving God.

Establish a Foundation of Faith

She said:

Our kids don't just learn things automatically or by osmosis. Here's an example. Several years ago, at the booksellers' convention in Atlanta, Larry and I met a woman who was the principal of an inner-city school in a predominantly black community. She told us something shocking: when the eighth graders at her school were assigned to write an essay on the contributions of Dr. Martin Luther King Jr., it was discovered that 80 percent of the students had never heard of him. How could that be, you ask? It comes down to parents neglecting to pass on truths and values to their children.

Parents have a big responsibility when it comes to imparting wisdom and knowledge to their children. Where else are their kids going to hear what they need to know? Certainly not in the public schools. Probably not in their neighborhoods. Maybe not even in their Christian schools. Parents must be diligent in imparting wisdom to their children and molding their hearts so that they will grow in the ways of God.

We've said that the sign of a cursed nation is when sons don't know who their fathers are. The sad truth is, that is the case more often than not. It is more crucial now more than ever before that we know and remember who are spiritual fathers are, that we absorb their words, wisdom, traditions, and ideals, and that we pass along those things to our children, day and night. We need to pass them along by living them out, teaching by example how to return malice with kindness, how to turn wrongs into rights, and how to turn the other cheek. We are to reproduce the goodness of God toward our families and through them. The *shema* that we pray, that we live by.

The word *shema* means "to hear," and that doesn't mean it goes in one ear and out the other. It isn't background noise, such as elevator music, that you don't really hear. When we meditate on and talk about the things of God, we digest His Word, absorbing it like a sponge absorbs water, until it becomes who we are.

Your Children Are Listening, Even If It Doesn't Look That Way

From the time they were born, our children basically lived at the church. Sometimes, they slept through the service or made a masterpiece in their coloring books. But they somehow got the message, for when you least expected it, they would spout off something they'd internalized from a Sunday school lesson or a song. Just the other day, my grandson Asher, a first grader, said, "Nothing's impossible with our God." I thought, *Where did he get that?* In church, of course!

Our daughter Anna has a little dog that got sick, and her daughter, two-year-old Aviva, took the dog in her lap and said, "Don't worry, Roxy. God's going to heal you. He's going to take care of you." And then she laid hands on the dog and began to pray. Two years old! Children see and then do; they absorb and then become. They reproduce in kind.

Get Them There and Let God Do the Rest

When it comes to getting their kids to church, some parents prefer going easy on their kids, for fear of forcing anything down their kids' throats. A woman recently asked me on Facebook to address what parents can do to get their kids to church when the kids don't want to go. Let me ask a question: Do your kids go to school? Of course. Did you give them a choice? Did you let them decide whether they wanted an education? No. Because, if you gave them the choice, and they refused, you'd be in jail.

We're the custodians. We're the parents. If we don't send our children to school, we're delinquent, and we'll probably face criminal charges. How about immunizations? Did you give your kids the option to get immunized? No, you dragged them to the doctor's office, kicking and screaming, fighting and clawing, and made them get their shots. Parents need to be able to put their foot down and demand that their children follow where they lead.

When it comes to church, why are so many parents hesitant to use the same authority? Some say, "I don't want to force my children to come because I'm afraid they'll reject Christianity." Have they rejected learning? No. Once they got to school, they loved it. Have they rejected being free of disease? Having healthy teeth? Of course not. Do you let them off the hook just because they don't feel like doing something? Rarely. You're the parent, and you know what's best for them! Tell them, "You're a member of my family, and this is how we roll. We go to church, and you're coming along."

To a parent who says, "I don't want my kids to be turned off to Christianity," I respond, "Well, that's fine, but there's no chance they'll get turned on to it if they aren't coming to church." God will grab hold of their hearts, and we need to leave that to Him. Our job is to get them in the door, so that the Holy Spirit can get ahold of their hearts.

It isn't as if I'm not speaking from experience. My kids each went through a phase, too. There were times when, as teenagers, they wanted to disengage from church activities because other things were calling for their attention. It was up to Larry and me to put our foot down and say, "You're coming to church. You're going to be a leader. And you're going to have a great attitude about it. When I see you up in the balcony, I'd better see you with hands raised, praising the Lord, not whispering to your neighbor."

> *Our job is to get them in the door, so that the Holy Spirit can get ahold of their hearts.*

As Larry likes to say, the consequences were worse than raising their hands and being embarrassed in front of their friends.

Yes, there were a few times when we had to make an adjustment—when our kids needed to repent and turn in a different direction. But, as their mother, I wasn't just going to sit back and say, "Oh, you know kids. They're just sowing their wild oats. It's okay for them to lose interest in serving God during their teenage years." No! In our house, we upheld a standard. "Everybody else is doing such and such," they'd sometimes whine. My response? "We aren't everybody else! Our spiritual fathers and mothers did it this way, and we will, too. If you're living in this house, this is how we roll. No buts about it."

Guess what? It worked! And they are better for it. My kids still love Jesus, and they still love Mom and Dad. We're best friends, really. But we had to help them along the path. Someone might ask, "What if I force my kids to serve God, and they rebel?" If we don't force them in this lifetime, we can rest assured they won't have a chance to serve Him in hell. If you get them to church in this life, they've got a chance because they'll hear the Word, which is a seed that gets planted in their hearts. Remember what I said before about my grandchildren regurgitating Bible verses and biblical truths out of the blue? They're like sponges. They absorb everything. Once we get it inside of them, it becomes real.

I like to use the illustration of building a concrete wall. If you're going to build a concrete wall, you can't pour out some concrete and expect it to stand up as a wall. It will be a messy heap. If you want a wall, you've got to build a structure for it—a fake structure, maybe out of wood. Then, you pour the concrete in. When the concrete hardens, you can remove the support system.

The same process applies in shaping our kids' spirits. We've got to give them a structure into which God can pour the "concrete" of His love and wisdom. When it hardens and becomes real, we can remove the "fake" structure, and our children's faith will stand on its own.

He said:

Some parents ask, "What if I force my kids to come to church and I end up pushing them away from the faith?" If they are away from the church, they're already away from the faith—you're just making sure they stay there. But, when you bring them to church, they hear the Word, which will not return to God void. (See Isaiah 55:11.) Maybe they don't want to be in God's house—fine. But God's Word will not return to Him void. It will remain in them. And then, when their friends start to lead them in a different direction, His voice will always be there, beckoning them back.

One way to make this a reality in the life of your kids is to seek out a church where the leaders, particularly those involved in ministering to children, youth, and young adults, are skilled at planning age-appropriate activities that are at the same time engaging and instructive. When our kids understand that learning about God and having fun are not mutually exclusive activities, they'll be more likely to retain what they learn, as well as to want to share it with others.

Keys for Raising Christ-Centered Kids

She said:

Nothing is automatic. But there are some things that we've learned and implemented in our child-raising efforts that have worked, and we want to share them with you.

Emphasize a Personal Salvation Experience

Even if a child has grown up in the church—even if he or she was raised reading the Word of God, hearing sermons preached on a regular basis, and seeing lives changed—he or she should have a personal, firsthand encounter with God. All of our children can point to a time when the Lord did something specific in their lives, and they said, "I want to be saved."

I remember when it happened to Anna, our oldest. She was five. We were living in Australia at the time. On this particular day, we were baptizing a group of former drug addicts in the ocean. All of a sudden, little Anna blurted out, "I want to give my life to the Lord." The older kids were giving their testimonies—"I was on drugs," "I was in a gang," and so forth—and little Anna steps up to the microphone and says, "I was a liar...I stoled." (She had never stolen anything.) But she realized the importance of giving a testimony, and she wanted to share her own. And then, the Spirit of God came upon her, and she started weeping. Moments later, Larry baptized her in the ocean, and, from that moment on, Anna had a real relationship with the Lord. It was no longer "Mommy and Daddy's church" or "Mommy and Daddy's God."

From that moment on, her faith was not about a bunch of do's and don'ts; it was about a determination to be different. At school, she committed to being a light to her classmates. Committed to taking Jesus with her. I remember her first year of school, how scared she was. We prayed that the Lord would go with her, and, I'm telling you, God changed her from the inside out.

Each one of our children has had a similar experience. Each one of them had to meet the Lord firsthand and come to Him of their own volition. And Larry and I never pushed our kids into the ministry. We just let them do what was in their heart and grow into the men and women God designed them to be.

Lead Your Children in Prayer and Bring God's Promises to Life

We have to be intentional about helping our children to build a relationship with the Lord. Larry and I tried to remain sensitive to our kids' spiritual growth, always looking for opportunities to invite them to pray. If I saw God moving in them, I would say, "Come on, let's go pray. God is doing something special in your life right now." These times were turning points—entrance portals, or open doors, for the Holy Spirit.

From the time our kids were young, we tried to help them connect to the promises of God and to experience His love in their own lives. Rather than simply telling them, we helped them to experience change from the inside out, so that they would do the right thing not out of a sense of obligation but because they wanted to please God (and their parents, too).

Set Spiritual Boundaries

According to the Barna Group, nearly half of all Americans who accept Jesus Christ as Lord and Savior do so before the age of thirteen.[6] Why is this important? Because it means that our children are the most malleable in their formative years. During this time of life, they are the most vulnerable to the influences of the secular world, yes, but they're also equally sensitive to the Spirit of God.

The Barna survey also said that two of every three born-again Christians made a commitment to Christ before their eighteenth birthday; that those who become Christians early on, before reaching their teenage years, are more likely to remain committed to their faith throughout their life than are those who came to Christ during or after their teenage years; and that Americans who embraced Christ during high school or college are less likely than other believers to describe themselves as "deeply spiritual."[7]

So, you see, the sooner you grab them, hook them, and train them, the better the chances of their remaining committed to the Lord for life. Do you know why that encourages me? Because we have a fighting chance to expose them to the gospel and to get them plugged into God's Word before the world causes them to stray from the path.

---

[6] http://www.barna.org/barna-update/article/5-barna-update/196-evangelism-is-most-effective-among-kids.
[7] Ibid.

Get Your Children Connected at Church

I know that many parents struggle with getting their kids connected in the church and, even more so, with keeping them connected. It definitely takes some effort on the part of parents. We expected our children to be involved, but we actively involved them.

At our church, New Beginnings, all of our kids are on staff—not because their name is Huch, but because we raised them to be a part of what we were doing, and they stuck with it. In our thirty-five years of ministry, our kids have always played a vital role. Whether they were sticking flyers on cars or spreading the word in other ways about the seven churches we've pioneered, they've always been instrumental in our work for the kingdom. In fact, our kids were basically our staff for a while. Larry would be up front preaching; I would sit at the organ with Anna beside me and pound out three chords. Every once in a while, I would call over my shoulder for her to stop wandering around and come sit back down.

> *When we get our children connected to the church and in community with God's people, great things happen.*

We were a one-man show for a number of years. Finally, Anna grew old enough to run the nursery—two's plenty mature, right? Luke was the head usher when he was one and a half, and Katie has been the boss ever since she could talk. By the grace of God, we've managed to keep our kids involved in church, and we've grown together spiritually as a family. I have a wonderful marriage and a loving family, all thanks to the goodness of God.

One of the greatest investments we can make in the lives of our children is to facilitate their spiritual growth through involvement at church.

Prioritize Church Activities

I realize that there are a lot of activities that conflict with events and programs at church. Yet church is the most important place we can take our children. Sports, dance lessons, music lessons, and other activities are great, but when we get our children connected to the church and in community with God's people, great things happen.

I talked in an earlier chapter about the importance of exposing our children to the highest form of their interests—taking them to concerts, museums, and the like. But, above all, let's get them to church! In most cases, there is a staff of people who love nothing more than nurturing young people in the ways of the Lord. They want to partner with parents, and parents would be wise to accept their help.

Larry and I have always prioritized church activities above any other options our kids were given. For example, we always had church on Wednesday nights, and the kids had to forfeit participation in certain sports and other activities as a result. I remember having to pull Luke out of T-ball because it started meeting on Wednesday nights. But we made sure to emphasize what he was gaining in return—the blessings of faithfulness from God. Our kids have always been intimately involved in what we're doing, and they have been instrumental in creating and improving ministries and programs for the youth. It's crucial to involve our kids in a way that they see their involvement becomes a fun adventure.

Of course, their participation will be what they make of it. We always told our kids, "You have to be involved, but the choice to have your heart involved is yours." Thank the Lord, they've stayed on that path, and their hearts have always been involved. They've always been soulwinners who have stayed plugged into the church. One primary reason for this is, I believe, because their hearts have been in it. We taught them how to have a relationship of love and intimacy with the Lord. It's about much more than merely coming to church.

Discover the Blessings of Observing *Shabbat* with Your Family

He said:

If you don't have a church service you typically attend on Friday nights, you might consider observing *Shabbat* with your family. *Shabbat* is a supernatural practice.

Now, some people get nervous when they hear the word "supernatural." Yet most of them probably experience the supernatural on a daily basis! Is it supernatural to lift up your hands in praise? It is, because the Lord inhabits the praises of His people. (See Psalm 22:3 KJV.) Is it supernatural to lay hands on someone who needs healing and to come into agreement with the promises of God? It sure is. Is it supernatural to anoint someone with oil? Is it supernatural to have the power of life and death in your tongue? (See Proverbs 18:21.) Absolutely.

In *Shabbat*, God just takes us one step further into the supernatural. On Fridays, if you're working when the sun starts to set, stop immediately and say,

"I'm coming into agreement with what God says about my children, not with what the world says about them." Every Friday, wherever you are, come into agreement with the Word as you speak over your children. Tiz and I speak over Brandin and Anna; Luke and Jen; Katie and her future husband; Asher, Judah, and Aviva; and so forth, asking that they might bring honor to the Lord and fulfill the destinies He has planned out for them.

Ancient Jewish wisdom says that the moment our children were conceived, they stood before the throne of God, and He gave them a destiny to change the world. It doesn't matter what they are going through right now; God gave them a destiny to be the light of the world and the salt of the earth. But the world's telling them differently. So, on Friday night, we walk into the Sabbath rest, or *menucha*, of God—His peace, blessings, prosperity, victory, joy, health, and happiness—and we prophesy over our children. We say, "May our sons and grandsons be like Ephraim and Manasseh, who, even though they were born outside the Promised Land, always walked in the Word and in the promises of God." We say, "May our daughters be great women of God, like Rebekah, Sarah, Rachel, and Leah. Father, may they bring honor to Your name and honor to our family name." And then, we cover our children with long life and divine blessing, destiny, and prosperity.

From Friday night through Sunday, we allow no arguing in the house. No negative words are to be spoken; no problems may be discussed. Victory alone is what we speak, because there is death and life in the power of the tongue. (See Proverbs 18:21.) We don't talk about how our children messed up. We don't discuss anything negative that happened at school. We talk about their divine destinies, which are covered by the blood of Jesus. This special night can heal many of the hurts our family members may have sustained during the week. It is a time when we take a break from "normal," day-to-day life and rest awhile in the peace of God.

Practice What You Preach

Kids are observant and insightful. If they see their parents come to church on Sunday morning and lift their hands in praise and worship, only to go home and spend Sunday afternoon cheating, lying, or gossiping, they'll know their parents' faith is fake or, at best, shaky. If children see their parents cheating in business or bragging about taking advantage of others, for example, they'll see right through any phony spiritual maturity. If we routinely gossip about the pastor and staff, it's no wonder our kids don't want to come to church! Children aren't going to want to serve God if their parents' spiritual life is not genuine. They'll call them "hypocrites"—and they'll be right.

Tiz and I have always committed to being the same people at home and behind the pulpit. Our kids can attest that whatever we say in church or on television is not an attempt to manipulate the congregation or hoodwink the viewing audience.

Leave a Legacy of Faith

In the book of Leviticus, God says, *"Therefore you shall keep My commandments, and perform them…I am the LORD who sanctifies you, who brought you out of the land of Egypt, to be your God"* (Leviticus 22:31–33). The word for *"sanctifies"* can also connote marriage, so we could also read verse 32 as saying, "I am the Lord who marries you." God says, "This is the reason I saved you—not just so that you would be saved, but so that you could pass along salvation."

What if our faith had stopped with Tiz and me? What if it stops with you? We are one generation away from not serving God if we don't pass on our faith to the children He has given us to raise. The media—movies, talk shows, pop songs—are all saying the same thing: "We don't care about kids." The idea of abortion used to be shocking, but we've grown accustomed to hearing about the practice. And the divorce rate among Christians is just as high as it is in the world. Our children aren't serving God. All of this is a part of Satan's plan, the strategy he's had in place from Egypt on to get the parents to stop rather than pass along their spiritual legacy.

But God says, "This is why I saved you—so that you might pass it on." And we must take a stand. We have to say, "Raising kids is a tough job, but it's tougher to raise a baby out of wedlock. It's tougher to have children who are addicted to drugs. It's tougher to have children in prison."

Don't Worry About Being "Super-Spiritual"

Do you know why I serve God? It isn't because I'm afraid of going to hell. I serve God because He gives me life—abundant live. Joy unspeakable. And so, when we were raising our children, we would say, "Why would you not serve God? The enemy's out there to steal, kill, and destroy. God's here to give us life, joy, happiness, and peace." So, they had that foundation.

I'll say this to parents, especially new parents: No matter how tired you are, never decide that you're too tired to pray with your kids before they go to sleep. We don't need to be "super-spiritual." Jesus wasn't super-spiritual. Sometimes, we can turn our children off to the things of God when we try to act super-spiritual. Watching cartoons with our kids may not seem spiritual, but it's one way of fulfilling our biblical mandate. The important thing is to be yourself as you lead your children to experience the love of God.

> *We can turn our children off to the things of God when we try to act super-spiritual.*

It's Never Too Late

There is no greater power in the world than the blood of Jesus, and by His blood, we can break every curse right now. Whether our children are three or thirty, we can say, "As for me and my family, we will serve the Lord." No matter the ages of our children, it's never too late to start praying for them, to witness to them, and to tell them what's right and wrong—not in a condemning way, of course, but in a way that will lead them and guide them, for God says that His Word will not return to Him void. (See Isaiah 55:11.) It's never too late to plead the blood of Jesus over them.

Do you want to know why I am saved today? Everybody told my mom and dad, "Your kid's a drug addict. Once a junkie, always a junkie." When I got saved, I was hitting up heroin and cocaine ten to twelve times a day, living in a shack with no heat, because I'd sold everything to keep my drug addiction going. And everybody said, "That's it. He can't change. Kid's a junkie. Once a junkie, always a junkie."

The world says, "Look at your child; look at your grandchild; look at you— you'll never change." The world says, "You can't change," but the Word of God says, "If the Son sets you free, you are free indeed." (See John 8:36.) I am saved today because of my Jewish aunt Helen, who loved Jesus with all her heart. In the middle of a drug deal, right before I found out that there was a warrant out for my arrest, I checked the mail and found a Bible. I had long hair, earrings, needle marks up and down my arms. My aunt said, "God told me this was your time. It's time for you to come to Jesus."

Aunt Helen was ninety-eight when she left this earth. On her deathbed, she still loved the Lord, and she was still a fireball. She'd been staying with my mom, and she said, "Ida, come here." My mom said, "What do you want, Helen?" Aunt Helen said, "Get my purse." My mom thought she was getting senile, so she said, "What do you want your purse for?" "I am going home." Mom replied, "Helen, you can't go anywhere; you're too weak." Yet Aunt Helen insisted, "I'm going home." Mom said, "What do you mean?" "He's coming! I am going home."

Mom asked again why she wanted her purse, and she said, "I want to give one more offering for the kids." She understood the process of atonement we just talked about. Then, she said, "I want you to tell the kids to do the same. Tell them not to buy any flowers—I'm going to heaven, and the flowers on earth can't even compare to the flowers in heaven." She said, "I want you to have the kids go to church, give an offering, and tell the Lord, 'Thank You.'" So, she wrote a check, handed it to my mom, and said, "Give this to my pastor." With that, she closed her purse and said, "I'm going home now. You be good. I'll see you when you get home." Then, she said, "There He is. Yeah, I'm ready."

Points to Ponder and Apply

+ Cultivate your children's personal relationship with God, and be sensitive to their spiritual questions.

+ Get your children plugged in at church—in ministry, as well as in volunteer roles that match their gifts.

+ Make Sunday service a priority for your family. If your kids have friends sleeping over, take them along with you!

+ Incorporate the Word of God into your daily conversation.

Chapter 11

REVERSING THE CURSE AND UNLEASHING THE BLESSING

Every adversity, every failure, every heartache carries with it the
seed of an equal or greater benefit.
—Napoleon Hill

She said:

Larry and I have had to overcome many of the same issues other people face. When we got married, he was still dealing with an anger problem, as well as a rather tumultuous history. He had to learn how to give love—as well as to receive it. He needed to have the curse of violence broken off of his life, and the process was gradual. At various points in our early years of marriage, the issue manifested, and we needed to deal with it time and again. A major turning point was when Larry lost his temper and shoved Luke, who was just a little boy at the time. It was a wake-up call for Larry. He stepped back and realized, *I'm just like my father. I need to stop this.* That's when we started to learn about generational curses—or, as the world calls them, "negative family patterns."

As human beings under the curse of Adam, we all have a driving force of iniquity that prompts us to commit sinful acts. And the iniquity is what we defeat when we break generational curses, severing them by the power of the blood of Jesus.

For example, a family may have a history of alcoholism or another type of addiction. To break that curse, it's necessary to sever the spirit of addiction that has been compelling people to succumb to those addictions.

Often, when we are dealing with an issue, it's because we have a curse on us that we aren't even aware of. One time, while I was up in Montana visiting my family, I found out about some things that went on in past generations that I hadn't known about before, including bootlegging and cattle rustling. You wouldn't believe how grateful I was to get those curses broken off of my life!

Then, there were the issues I'd already known about. When I was growing up, my siblings and I were very close to all of our cousins, and my mom made sure that we all spent time together. She thought it important that we know all of our grandparents, aunts, and uncles—everybody. Without mentioning any names, there was one branch of the family with really neat people, but they were alcoholics. I'm not talking casual drinkers; they had severe alcohol addictions. And the mother had the worst case. Her children, my cousins, were always embarrassed by her behavior when she was intoxicated, which was most of the time. We'd have a family event, and she would show up falling-down drunk and just embarrass everybody, and the kids hated it. I can remember sitting with my cousins as they cried. One of them said, "I'm so embarrassed. I can't stand the way she acts."

Years later, this girl turned into her mother. The behavior she had once hated and resented became the very behavior that defined her later in life. She had inherited a generational curse. Even before I knew about the reality of generational curses, I knew the process of learned behavior being passed down. My cousin had learned that the way to have fun was to drink and party. The only way of life she knew was the life her parents had modeled to her and her siblings. Thank the Lord, she sought counseling later on and got her life turned around. But there was a spiritual change and an intentional behavioral change that were necessary.

He said:

Therefore you shall lay up these words of mine in your heart and in your soul, and bind them as a sign on your hand, and they shall be as frontlets between your eyes. You shall teach them to your children, speaking of them when you sit in your house, when you walk by the way, when you lie down, and when you rise up. And you shall write them on the doorposts of your house and on your gates, that your days and the days of your children may be multiplied in the land of which the LORD swore to your fathers to give them, like the days of the heavens above the earth. (Deuteronomy 11:18–21)

This passage from Deuteronomy is talking about the blessing of the father being passed down to the third and fourth generations after him. We know that blessings—and curses, too—are passed down from mothers and fathers to their children, grandchildren, great-grandchildren, and so forth. If Dad is lazy, there's a good chance his children will be lazy, too. If Mom is negative, there's a good chance her kids will also be negative. But the good thing is that we can break those curses!

Breaking Generational Curses

She said:

Generational curses come in all shapes and sizes—alcoholism, anger, depression, poverty, divorce, and so forth. And they are passed on from generation to generation, unless we step in and sever those curses in the spiritual realm.

Know Your Family History

It's a common occurrence for us to be praying for someone who is going through a divorce, for example, and to find out that there is a history of divorce in the family. At that point, we break the curse of divorce. We cast out the spirit of division and discord, which tries to creep up in marriages and cause havoc. In some cases, we ourselves, not our ancestors, have ushered in the curse, and we need to go in and sever the spiritual root that is causing us to act in a particular way. Someone who is prone to addictions, outbursts of anger, or mood swings, for example, needs to uproot the curse of iniquity that's pulling him or her toward those behaviors. That's the wonderful thing about breaking generational curses—the result is spiritual, emotional, and physical freedom.

Some natural behaviors have natural results. Someone who just happens to be mean and grouchy is going to encounter consequences in marriage, as well as in every relationship, that didn't result from a curse.

Breaking family curses is a spiritual practice, but it has a natural side, as well. This is where our free will comes in—our personal choices and decisions. For example, in some cases, divorce is just a consequence of behavior and circumstances, rather than something that's been passed down through a curse. Some natural behaviors have natural results. Someone who just happens to be a mean, grouchy person is going to encounter consequences in marriage, as well as in every relationship, that didn't result from a curse.

So, the approach must be twofold—spiritual and natural. We break curses in the spiritual realm and modify behavior in the natural realm.

The Bible says that many are called, but few are chosen. (See Matthew 22:14 KJV, NKJV.) There are many interpretations of this particular Scripture, but I believe that one of the meanings is that God puts His call out to every one of us—He throws the ball—and those of us who decide to catch it become chosen ones. The promise of blessings is ours, if we will only activate that promise by taking ownership of it. We have to make right choices!

This principle applies not only to our marriages and our relationships with our kids but to all aspects of life. There's the spiritual part—God's supernatural promises and blessings—and there's the natural part—our part. These realms intersect when we activate God's promises by breaking curses and severing spiritual strongholds. We go in and we clean house, spiritually, and then our focus turns to the natural as we learn new behavior patterns.

Establish New, Healthy Patterns

The Lord wants to give us wisdom and discernment as we walk through the process of breaking family curses. Sometimes, an established pattern is not necessarily the right or best way to do something. I'll illustrate with this story. A newlywed bride wanted to cook her new husband a nice meal. So, she went out and bought a beautiful cut of beef to make pot roast. Her husband watched her prepared the meal. As she was preparing to place the meat in the pan, she chopped the ends off of the roast and threw them in the trash. Her husband protested, saying, "Honey, why are you throwing away perfectly good meat?" Defensively, she replied, "That's the way you make a roast." "Really?" he asked. "Yes, of course. That's the way my mother did it, and that's the way her mother did it. That's how it's done." He said, "Well, I've never seen it done that way." To prove him wrong, the wife called up her mom and said, "Mom, I'm making a roast, and I chopped off the ends, just as you always did. Isn't that the way to make a roast?" Her mom laughed and replied, "Oh, honey, the only reason I did that was, my pan was too small."

See? Even something that's done "the way it should be" isn't always right or necessary. All of those old television shows depicting husbands and wives demeaning each other—Archie Bunker, Roseanne, and so forth—are hardly a model to follow. Men need to be respected and honored, not put down. Wives need to be valued and revered, not demeaned. Morals aside, the way we interact with one another is truly a determinant in the course of our families' futures! Maybe it's "always been done that way." Maybe your dad treated your mom with condescension. Maybe your mom patronized your dad. In my family, it was normal for the wife to boss her husband around. But that isn't right. Let's work on godly behavior!

Don't Nourish the Curse with Negative Words

One obstacle to the process of breaking curses is declaring negative things about our families. I know someone who is always saying things like, "I have the worst marriage," "I'm ready to trade in my husband," and "My kids are such a mess." But using negative words is not the way to bring positive change to her situation, because her words are only reinforcing what she doesn't want for her family. The Bible teaches that *"death and life are in the power of the tongue"* (Proverbs 18:21). This woman's words speak death to her family! We need to change the course of our words if we hope to change the course of our families and relationships.

Avoid Common Curses

Premarital Sex/Fornication

I have met new Christians, and even some seasoned ones, who are surprised when they find out that the Bible prohibits sexual relations until marriage. I've counseled women who have had babies out of wedlock who have told me that their parents never said, "Wait until you're married." If that's the case, then an important family value has not been established. Unless something changes, and unless the children in these families are trained in this particular realm, then the chance of children being born out of wedlock increases drastically. It may be the twenty-first century, but some things never change. And that includes the sinfulness of premarital sex.

He said:

You probably know someone whose grandmother got pregnant out of wedlock, whose mother got pregnant out of wedlock, and whose daughter got pregnant out of wedlock. This is a curse that brings many consequences, both natural and spiritual, on a family! And a curse doesn't just come; a curse abounds. When people have sexual relations outside of wedlock, and an "unwanted" pregnancy results, the couple may decide to have an abortion—a practice that has reached epidemic proportions in the world. When our nation began to lose its traditional values and became more accepting of immoral practices for the sake of convenience, the practice of killing babies became almost commonplace. Remember, God's people value life and make choices to protect it at all costs!

> *When we walk with conviction and obey the Lord, we'll see miracles in our families and live the abundant life God intends for us.*

Here's the key: Don't have sex before you're married. Sex isn't bad—it's a good gift from God, *when it is practiced in the context of marriage.* The Bible says that the marriage bed is undefiled. (See Hebrews 13:4.)

Let me say this, too: Don't marry a man unless he's serving God and working a job that pays the bills! If he doesn't meet those criteria, don't even date him. God has a wonderful plan for your life and your family—a plan that includes joy, peace, and happiness—but He needs you to take a stand and say, "I'm breaking this curse off of my family." When we walk with conviction and obey the Lord, we'll see miracles in our families and live the abundant life God intends for us. (See John 10:10.)

Unforgiveness

Curses can also result from unforgiveness. If you're married, and you're harboring a grudge against your spouse, let it go. How would we like to have Jesus bring up every mistake we've ever made? Unforgiveness opens the door to all kinds of problems in marriage and in life. As Tiz always says, unforgiveness is like drinking poison and expecting someone else to get sick.

God commands us to forgive. He even says He won't forgive us if we don't forgive others. (See Matthew 6:14–15.) The act of forgiveness is one of the most powerful tools available to us as we seek to remove those things that are blocking our blessings. If you need healing, whether in a physical, emotional, or spiritual sense, and if you want to experience a sense of wholeness and freedom, you need to let some things go. When you do this, the power of God will flow through you as never before.

Let's pray right now: "Father, forgive me for not forgiving. From this moment on, in my family, I will be the peacemaker, not the troublemaker, in Jesus' name."

Okay, it's done. "But, Pastor Larry," you might say, "I don't feel like it's done." Remember, your feelings are real, but they aren't the truth. When you make a decision to forgive and speak forgiveness, you shouldn't allow your brain to continue thinking about it when it's done. Stand in faith that your feeling will follow your decision. Don't allow Satan to come in and steal your blessing by convincing you that forgiveness hasn't taken place. Choose today to forgive.

Speak and Sever the Curses

She said:

We have the opportunity to be an example that will cause the world to desire our God. The success that we experience in our relationships with our spouses, children, and grandchildren is a powerful testimony for the Lord. We want our homes to be safe havens—peaceful retreats for our spouses and children, away from the enemy and his schemes. So, let's break every curse off of our homes, our marriages, and our families. Maybe you've gone through a bad marriage or two—or four or five. Let's break that curse. We have only one earthly life. Let's make it the best—and the most blessed—it can be.

Maybe you are realizing that you have some baggage you brought to your marriage, baggage you see manifesting itself in your children. Join the club! We're all in this together. But, together, we want to reverse the curse and release the blessing over our lives, so that we can begin moving down a better path.

Let me ask you to do something right now. Whether you're single or married, I want you to stand in your living room and say, "I break every curse that may be in this house or on my life, especially any curses I may have brought forth through my words. I cover my marriage and my children right now with the blessings of God."

My hope is that, once you've prayed this prayer, God will open your eyes, and you will feel as if your entire house has been cleansed—as if every wall has been given a fresh coat of paint.

Releasing Generational Blessings

Larry and I believe strongly in the importance of releasing generational blessings—legacies that we pass along to our children, our children's children, and so forth. In this case, the opposite of generational curses occurs: we release into our children a desire to do right, a passion to serve God. Remember, Christianity isn't about a list of do's and don'ts. It's about a transformation on the heart level—a change from the inside out.

We will not allow our children to inherit whatever curses may have come upon us from our ancestors. Rather, we will release to our children, to our children's children, and to their children the blessings of God and the benefits of a godly life. I cannot overstate the significance of this process.

We are dealing with behaviors that can usher in either a generational curse or a generational blessing. I don't know about you, but I'm going down the blessing path. We've learned how to break the curse—now, let's learn how to release the blessing. Let's get in there, perform a "checkup from the neck up," and change any behaviors that may be contributing to the continuation of a curse so that we can set a good example for our children and establish a healthy, wholesome pattern for them to follow.

During a political campaign, the candidates always make lofty promises about how, if elected, they're going to change the world. Our world is in desperate need of change. Fine. But, sometimes, it seems as if the situation is pretty hopeless. Despite the attempts of well-meaning politicians, no single person or organization is capable of effecting true, lasting change in this world. This is why we need the Messiah.

Don't get me wrong—we need to vote; we need to participate in man-made aid efforts. But, above all, the world needs God. And the greatest thing we can do to participate in worldwide transformation is to change our families for the better. We really can change the world by changing our families. You and I can be the generation that stops family curses in their tracks. We can break generational patterns of destruction and create a new world by releasing generational blessings into the lives of our children.

When your kids are grown, as ours are, you find yourself wondering where the time went. Thank the Lord we learned how to break generational curses in order to stop those negative recurring patterns in our own lives, as well as in the lives of our children and grandchildren.

Honoring Parents Unleashes the Blessing

He said:

Deuteronomy 5:16 says, *"Honor your father and your mother, as the LORD your God has commanded you, that your days may be long, and that it may be well with you in the land which the LORD your God is giving you."*

What if I told you that honoring your parents is one key to removing whatever's blocking the blessing from your life? Let's see what happens when we rewrite that Scripture in a negative sense: "Don't honor your father and your mother, and your days will not go well, and you won't be around for very long."

Now, I want to throw in a little something that freaks me out sometimes. You are probably familiar with the method of exacting justice in the Old Testament, which we summarize as "eye for eye, tooth for tooth." (See Exodus 21:23–25.) For every wrong action, there was a corresponding penalty, but in the Hebrew, it has more to do with how God reacts. He didn't mean that if you lost an eye, you ought to go and pluck out somebody else's eye. That might be what the person deserves, but God is a merciful God, and so it isn't going to happen.

Likewise, when the Bible says, *"Honor your father and your mother…that your days may be long,"* it doesn't mean that God is going to kill you if you don't. But if we fail to honor our father and mother, it isn't going to go well for us—God will make sure of it.

God said to Moses, *"Speak to all the congregation of the children of Israel, and say to them: 'You shall be holy, for I the* LORD *your God am holy. Every one of you shall revere his mother and his father, and keep My Sabbaths: I am the* LORD *your God'"* (Leviticus 19:2–3).

Deuteronomy 5:16 and Leviticus 19:2–3 are nearly identical Scriptures, but there is a key difference. Do you notice it? Look at the placement of the words "father" and "mother." As you can see, they are reversed in Deuteronomy 5:16 ("Honor your father and mother") and Leviticus 19:2–3 ("Honor your mother and father"). This means that we are to treat our parents with equal reverence. Instead of treating Mom one way and Dad a different way, we treat them with equal reverence.

In Hebrew, the word for *"honor"* has physical implications, while *"reverence"* is more of a spiritual act. So, while we revere our parents with our attitudes and words, we honor them in tangible ways—making sure they are fed, clothed, and housed; assuring that they get the proper care, especially in old age. We reverence them by refusing to patronize them, to talk back to them, to disgrace them, to embarrass them, and so forth.

Our reward for honoring our parents comes in this life, here on earth, while our compensation for reverencing them arrives via blessings in the afterlife.

Now, watch this. If we don't honor and reverence our parents, we bring a curse upon ourselves. And it goes both ways: We are to honor and reverence our own parents, as well as to make sure our children honor and reverence us. The respect or lack thereof will reap blessings or curses, accordingly. As parents, we need to set an expectation that our kids will respect us. We need to teach them

> *When we walk with conviction and obey the Lord, we'll see miracles in our families and live the abundant life God intends for us.*

to say "Please" and "Thank you" and to teach them not to cuss.

I don't know about you, but when I was a kid running the streets, I learned how to cuss. It wasn't long before I learned the consequences: eating Ivory soap. "If you're going to say dirty words, I'm going to wash your mouth out!" was my mom's threat. Today, I'm better for it.

When you're in the grocery store, and there's a kid who's being a brat, it's the parent who ought to be spanked. "Well, I have a high-strung child," the parent might say. My response is, "No, you just aren't doing what you're supposed to be doing! You need to teach your child to honor and respect you."

The "Bridge" of the Fifth Commandment

A deeper reason why the practice of honoring one's parents is so important is found in the Ten Commandments. The Ten Commandments are referred to by that name only twice in the original Hebrew, but they are called the "two tablets" thirty times. Why did God choose to list everything we ever really needed to know on just two tablets? Because, as I've said before, everything God does, He does two ways—there's always a physical component and a spiritual component.

The first four commandments have to do with our relationship with God: (1) we are to have no other gods before Him, (2) we are not to make graven images of Him, (3) we are not to take the Lord's name in vain, and (4) we are to remember the Sabbath and observe it. (See Exodus 20:3–10.) The final four commandments are about our relationships with other people. They say, "Thou shalt not..." (6) murder, (7) steal, (8) commit adultery, (9) bear false witness against your neighbor, or (10) covet your neighbors' possessions. (See Exodus 20:13–16.)

The fifth commandment bridges the gap between our relationship with God and our relationship with people: "You shall honor your father and your mother." (See Exodus 20:12.) Ancient wisdom teaches that if our children learn how to honor their fathers and mothers, they will experience blessings in their relationships with other people, as well as their relationship with God. Why is this? Because honoring our parents teaches us how to honor people with authority over us, including God.

Respect for One's Parents Parallels Respect for the Lord

I was talking to my friend Rabbi Lapin about this, and he made a comment that struck me. He said that they're the Ten Commandments, not the "Ten Suggestions." Following them is mandatory if we want to be successful in life. The *Talmud* teaches that learning to honor one's parents is the foundation of being successful in life and having meaningful interactions with society.

Let me share an example. Proverbs 3:9 says, *"Honor the* LORD *with your possessions, and with the firstfruits of all your increase."* It isn't enough just to say, "We love You, Lord." God says, "If you say you love Me but you don't love your neighbor, you don't really love Me." This is why we tithe. This is why we give. It's not enough to say, "I'm saved; I love You, Lord." He says, "If you love Me, go and tell the world." So, we honor the Lord with our possessions. Remember, the act of honoring implies a physical thing we act out here on earth, and it reaps blessings from God in this lifetime.

Leviticus 24:15–16 says, *"Then you shall speak to the children of Israel, saying: 'Whoever curses his God shall bear his sin. And whoever blasphemes the name of the* LORD *shall surely be put to death.'"* If we curse God, there's a spirit of death that will come upon us and every aspect of our lives. Jesus said, "You can curse Me, but if you blaspheme the Holy Spirit, watch out."

Exodus 21:17 says, *"He who curses his father or his mother shall surely be put to death."* Do you see the connection? There are serious consequences that stem from how we treat our parents.

Honor and Reverence Should Be Unconditional

When Rabbi Lapin was studying the Torah's teachings on honoring one's parents, he did an Internet search on court cases in which either a parent sued a child or a child sued a parent. What he discovered was that there were next to no cases of parents suing children, yet there were dozens of cases of children suing their parents. Plenty of kids were willing to throw their parents out of the house, but few parents forced their kids to leave home. And the reason, he surmised, was that he who gives much loves much.

In one particular case, a son owned the apartment complex where his parents resided, and he was trying to evict them. The judge told him, "What you're doing is legal, but it's wrong. I have to rule in your favor, but what you're doing—throwing your folks out in the street—is wrong." The son protested, saying, "How can it be wrong? They haven't paid the rent in sixty days." In other words, he was saying, "My parents don't deserve my honor." The commandment to honor our parents has nothing to do with whether they deserve it or not!

Some people say, "My parents never did anything for me." Really? They did nothing for you? You're here, aren't you? Yes? Well then, they brought you into this world—they are your physical creators. And if you won't honor them, you can't honor your spiritual Creator. These things go hand in hand!

National Blessings Hinge on the Hearts of Fathers and Children

After Jacob had wrestled with the Lord, he was told, "*Your name will no longer be Jacob, but Israel, because you have struggled with God and with men and have overcome*" (Genesis 32:28 NIV). After that, "*the sun rose above him…and he was limping because of his hip*" (verse 31 NIV).

Now, go with me to Malachi 4. The preceding chapter, Malachi 3, is about the financial blessings we will receive in return for our faithfulness with our tithes and offerings. Then, we read:

> "*For behold, the day is coming, burning like an oven, and all the proud, yes, all who do wickedly will be stubble. And the day which is coming shall burn them up,*" says the LORD of hosts, "*that will leave them neither root nor branch. But to you who fear My name The Sun of Righteousness shall arise with healing in His wings; and you shall go out and grow fat like stall-fed calves. You shall trample the wicked, for they shall be ashes under the soles of your feet on the day that I do this,*" says the LORD of hosts. "*Behold, I will send you Elijah the prophet before the coming of the great and dreadful day of the LORD. And he will turn the hearts of the fathers to the children, and the hearts of the children to their fathers, lest I come and strike the earth with a curse.*"
>
> (Malachi 4:1–6)

There is a prophecy unfolding here. It speaks of the fulfillment of the end-times transfer of wealth, which is summarized in Proverbs 13:22: "*The wealth of the sinner is stored up for the righteous.*" The "*Sun of Righteousness*" mentioned in Malachi 4 is also the Messiah, who is the third part of the menorah and who shall "*arise*" and heal your finances, so that you "*go out and grow fat like stall-fed calves.*"

The key to receiving the end-time transfer of wealth is with the fathers. We cannot have a relationship with the God who opens the windows of heaven and rebukes the devourer until, by the Spirit of God, God sends a prophet who teaches us how to turn the hearts of sons back to their fathers and the hearts of fathers back to their children. Remember, we aren't animals; we are the children of God!

God will never bless our finances to the fullest extent until we break the curse on our nation by bringing the hearts of the fathers back to their children and the hearts of the children back to their fathers. There's a curse on our nation that keeps males from being men. We need to be men! Let's get our backsides out of bed, go find ourselves a job, and start taking care of our wives and children. Anyone who is divorced and owes child support had better start paying, because God will never bless him until he does the right thing.

> I call heaven and earth as witnesses today against you, that I have set before you life and death, blessing and cursing; therefore choose life, that both you and your descendants may live; that you may love the LORD your God, that you may obey His voice, and that you may cling to Him, for He is your life and the length of your days; and that you may dwell in the land which the LORD swore to your fathers, to Abraham, Isaac, and Jacob, to give them.
> (Deuteronomy 30:19–20)

Choose life! Choose blessings!

Blessing or Curse: You Decide

We can choose to be happy, or we can choose to be miserable. We can choose to be full of life, or we can choose to be full of death. Whose choice is it? It's ours. However, if your parents or those in authority over you have said negative things to you or about you, you may be estranged from them right now. If so, yours is a broken relationship.

Praise God, there is hope! There is a way—God's way—to bring healing and blessing into our lives right now. Tiz and I have led many Freedom Weekends in our thirty-five-plus years of ministry, and we've prayed with multitudes of people to stop the cycle of broken relationships and to bring healing to broken hearts. We know, beyond a shadow of a doubt, that there can be restoration between adult children and their parents, no matter what it was that drove a wedge between them. If it was a negative word, it can be turned around.

PRAYER

Father, I come to You right now, in the name of Jesus. I know I've sinned. But I also know that You sent Your only Son, Jesus Christ, to pay the price in full for all of my sins. From this day on, You will not bring up any of my past mistakes. And, in Jesus' name, I will not bring up anyone else's past mistakes. Every curse on my home and my family is broken and reversed. My sons will be like Ephraim and Manasseh, and my daughters will be like Rebekah, Sarah, Rachel, and Leah. From this moment on, my family is covered by the blood of Jesus, so joy is mine, peace is mine, and blessings are mine, from today forward. It is done—it is sealed—in the mighty name of Jesus! Amen.

Points to Ponder and Apply

+ Establish healthy, biblical habits that promote life and success.

+ Speak those things that aren't as though they were: "My children are so loving and kind," "My marriage is great." You aren't lying; you are speaking in faith with the language of restoration.

+ Don't allow any unforgiveness to fester in your heart. Forgive your parents, your exes, your children, your friends, and yourself.

+ Honor your parents, both your biological parents and any spiritual mothers or fathers you may have.

+ Remember, the Ten Commandments are *commandments*, not suggestions.

Conclusion

LET YOUR LIGHT SHINE

She said:

L est you be tempted to think, *What difference can one little family make?* I'd like to tell you about a family who has experienced a ripple effect of generational blessings all because they've been obedient to follow God's plan.

Harold and Margaret, our good friends, were both raised in Christian homes, just as their parents and their grandparents before them had been, and they accepted Christ at a young age. They started attending our church more than twenty years ago and immediately got involved in church life, volunteering wherever help was needed. Their children, now grown (and still attending our church!), were in grade school at the time, and they, too, got involved helping, in children's ministry. Even when our church relocated to Texas, Harold and Margaret picked up and moved in order to remain a part of our family!

Over the years, they have remained committed to stepping up to meet the needs of God's people. Harold, Margaret, and their children—along with their children's spouses and children—have blessed thousands of lives. They are the type of family every pastor dreams of having in his church—people who will come alongside him and push toward the accomplishment of his God-given vision.

The amazing thing is that these traits aren't unique to Harold and Margaret. Their siblings have effected a similar impact on the kingdom of God, each one in his or her own way. For the past century, their family has produced five generations of strong, godly people who are bold in establishing God's dominion in the world. Among Harold and Margaret's siblings alone are three brothers who devoted a significant portion of their lives to missionary work in Africa. Another brother is the director of a large Christian denomination in Brazil. Many of their extended family members serve as police officers, civil servants, and military personnel, all of them ready to lay down their lives to keep their communities and nation safe. And hundreds of others in their family are prosperous businesspeople contributing to our nation's economy, as well as creating a model of godly marriages and Christ-centered families for their neighbors and fellow citizens to follow.

When our church expanded its food program to benefit children in Haiti, one of Harold and Margaret's sons and his wife, already the proud parents of three beautiful girls, adopted two additional children from our partner orphanage in Haiti. What a wonderful demonstration of the love of God in operation in a family!

The humble family after God's heart is truly a powerful key in His kingdom. Never underestimate your potential to change—and then to change the world, one family at a time. God wants to use your family in the same way He's using Harold and Margaret's. Will you take a stand? Will you be a light to lead others into the wonderful destiny God wants to give them?

Lights in a Darkening World

You are the light of the world. A city that is set on a hill cannot be hidden. Nor do they light a lamp and put it under a basket, but on a lampstand, and it gives light to all who are in the house. Let your light so shine before men, that they may see your good works and glorify your Father in heaven.

(Matthew 5:14–16)

People everywhere are starving for acceptance. In their search for validation, many of them pursue a course of destruction and end up missing all of the blessings God has in store for them. In our early years of ministry, we pastored young kids off the streets. A lot of them were addicted to drugs and other substances, but what they were really looking for wasn't drugs or immoral behavior; it was someone to validate them. Someone to tell them they were special. A place to fit in. They had found that in the world, or so they'd thought.

That's why it's so important that we, as members of the body of Christ, validate and affirm those God has placed along our path—family members, friends, neighbors, coworkers, and so forth. In our relationships with each other and in our homes, let's let the love of Jesus shine more brightly than ever before. Our marriages, our children, and our families need to shout to the world that God has a blessing for all those who will turn to Him—for those who will commit to following His path. Serving God and going to church are great, but the driving force of society is the family. It's up to us to raise the next generation to serve God and follow His ways.

Our marriages, our children, and our families need to shout to the world that God has a blessing for all those who will turn to Him.

Stay On Guard

Each of us has a will. It's up to us to choose to surrender and to stay on the path of obedience, so that we can move into the abundant life Jesus promised us. (See John 10:10.) Yet the world paints such an enticing picture. It pulls at every one of us, whether we're reading a magazine, watching TV, going to the movies, shopping at the mall, or interacting with our coworkers. We need a spiritual shower of the Word of God every day so that we won't be brainwashed by the habits and lifestyles of those who do not live according to God's blueprint.

Most of us are in the world, to some degree or another. We're out there working or getting together with friends. If these people are not followers of Jesus Christ, we need to make sure they aren't polluting us or influencing us with their values. We need to take hold of the Word of God and be living examples of the blessings that result from our standards and values. Let's make our lives living sermons. We don't have to preach at anybody; we just need to live in such a way that allows others to see the goodness of God. Then, if our friends' marriages start to fall apart or their kids are doing drugs, they'll look at us and say, *I wonder how I could have a life like that.* And that's when we can tell them about the hope we have in Jesus Christ. That's when we invite them to church and tell them that the power of God can turn their life around.

Again, the key is not to preach at them but to give them hope by *living* the hope. And we should make it positive: instead of saying, "If you do that, you'll face these consequences," we say, "If you do this, you'll get all of these benefits!" Now, that really is the good news!

Our God is not putting burdens on us. He's a burden-removing, yoke-destroying, all-powerful God. Let's call on Him as we break the curses off of our lives. Let's break any generational patterns of failure in marriage. Let's break those curses that try to grab our children and drag them into the world.

Tell Your Children to Take a Stand

He said:

Everywhere they go, our kids are going to meet people who invite them to smoke this or drink that. We need to be sure that they have an answer—something they know is far more valuable than anything the world has to offer, as Tiz talked about earlier. She said she never wanted to forfeit the fun and closeness she had with her family, and she credits that desire for keeping her on the straight and narrow as a young girl. Have a plan for your family, and be sure to do things together, to avoid leaving a void in your children's lives that they'll be tempted to fill with other, less wholesome activities.

Out there in the world, teenagers are getting pregnant, committing suicide, and dying of drug overdoses. It's an epidemic. And it's our job to be sure our kids have a different view on life and that they know how to share with their peers. The teenagers who are lost and searching are far more likely to listen to their peers and to follow their example than to listen to adults telling them what to do. The devil wants our kids to feel embarrassed about their faith. As their parents, we need to bolster their confidence and encourage them to reach out to others with the hope of the Lord, just as Tim Tebow and other Christian role models are doing.

> *The way I stayed saved was by telling everyone that I was a Christian. They didn't have to guess.*

When I got saved, I had been a drug addict who always hung around all the wrong folks. The way I stayed saved was by telling everyone that I was a Christian. They didn't have to guess. It got to the point where my friends would tell me, "You can come over, but you can't talk about Jesus anymore." I would respond, "I'm coming over, but you can forget the part about my keeping my mouth shut." And all of my friends got saved. At first, they didn't want to hear it, but if I hadn't made a stand, they wouldn't have made it in the world—or onto the next in eternity. One of my best friends passed away a couple of years ago. He was a football coach, and he had a heart attack. He'd gotten saved two years prior, and all because I'd decided to take a stand.

Let Your Light Shine

She said:

You and I are called by God to rise up as examples of His blessings on the home. It's obvious that the world needs some encouraging! Everywhere we go, we hear people voicing worries about their families. They're plagued by discord, arguments, divorce, troubled children, and so forth. But God has said to us, "I want to use your lives to set you apart. I want to use your lives to elevate you to a place where you can be an example of the godly homes I intended My people to have."

It's not easy to raise good, godly kids in this day and age. But it is possible. I'm not trying to brag, except to boast about what God has done for us as a way to build up your faith that He'll do it for you, too. Stand up and let your light shine!

Action Steps to Illuminate Your Light

Here are some great action steps for you to put into place right now, no matter where your family is or what condition it in.

For Your Family...

+ Keep your entire family in a good church. This isn't optional.

+ Don't say one thing in the church setting and then change your tune at home.

+ Be honest with your children about their qualities, but use words that are uplifting, not judgmental.

+ Be creative as you plan fun, frugal family activities. Having a good time together and creating meaningful memories does not need to be costly.

+ Be generous with your love. Every day, search for something specific to praise in each of your children.

+ When possible, affirm your children in front of your adult friends and family members. Make sure you praise them for who they are, not just for their performance.

+ Get to know your children's friends and keep tabs on the things they do together.

+ Establish clear-cut rules and regulations, and generously reward good behavior. Use positive reinforcement as much as possible.

+ Assign age-appropriate household chores to your children and teach them how to do the job right.

+ Include your children in conversations with your adult friends, not every time, but when appropriate.

+ Teach your children common courtesy. (While I think it shouldn't be necessary to list this, I think that this type of instruction has been forgotten by many parents.)

+ Let your children see you reading the Bible on a daily basis.

+ Pray for your children. Never let them leave the house without your saying a prayer of protection over them. Remember, your prayers need not be long and drawn out.

+ Celebrate the miracles God has done for your family and talk about them often, in order to build faith for the future.

For Your Marriage...

He said (to the men):

+ Let your children hear you praise your wife.

+ Prioritize family getaways, or simply time to spend exclusively with your family.

+ Be the protector. Let your wife and children know they can count on you.

+ Work a job, and don't spend all your time and money on your sports or activities

+ Laugh with your wife and children. Try to be fun to be around.

She said (to the women):

+ Schedule special date nights and romantic evenings with your husband.

+ Never speak negatively about your husband to anyone, especially your kids. Keep those conversations between you and God.

+ Lift up your husband with your words and actions. Remember, there are plenty of people who will tell him the "bad news"; it's your job to shower him with love, support, and affirmation.

+ Don't allow your children to occupy all of your time and energy. They should not come before your husband on your list of priorities.

+ Speak words of encouragement to your family, especially on *Shabbat*. God's ears are close to us on Friday nights, so be sure to speak life into every area of your home.

+ Learn to take your thoughts captive so that negativity doesn't ruin your day. Forgive and move on.

+ Try to say yes to your children as much as possible as you guide them and schedule their activities, even if the rest of the sentence may mean no.

Always remember that God want to bless you. He wants only good for you and your family. Today, start walking along the path He has set in place, and watch as He makes all blessings abound towards you and your family! Let's pray together.

Father, we give You praise and glory. You are all-powerful and everlasting. We stand in faith today, thanking You for the completed work of Jesus Christ on the cross at Calvary. Father, we release Your dominion and authority over our lives, as we declare that every place we put the soles of our feet, You give us dominion, and that everything we put our hand to, You will cause to prosper. We claim all of the generational blessings that are rightfully ours but have been held back by the enemy. Lord, release them now, through the blood of Jesus Christ.

Father, we put our foot down and proclaim that Satan has no dominion over our thoughts, our families, or our future. Release into our lives Your joy, peace, health, victory, favor, grace, anointing, and equipping. Thank You for giving us Your wisdom on how to love our spouses and children. Thank You for paying the price for our families to be whole.

We praise You, we worship You, and we give You all the glory, in Jesus' precious name. We declare nothing but the will of God in our lives, our families, and our homes. We repent of any words spoken, or deeds committed, outside of Your will. And we give to you any words spoken against us, because Jesus has paid the price for us to be healed and whole. Thank You for restoring any broken family relationships and for breathing life into the regions of our lives that were spiritually dead. Thank You for the power of Your Word and for Your unending love and grace. We ask You to raise us up as lights to our generation—beacons of hope in the world. In Jesus' name, amen.

•••

God bless you for taking the time to read this book and for making the effort to apply any wisdom you've gleaned to your life and family. No matter who you are or where you have come from, the Lord has a new beginning for you! What He has done for our marriage, family, and children, He is ready to do for yours, too. Every day is a new opportunity for you to take the steps to move forward on God's path of blessings. As you do, you can trust Him to give you strength, guidance, wisdom, and equipping to create a family filled with His blessings of love, joy, peace, and happiness! And you can also trust that pastors Larry and Tiz have you covered in prayer and wrapped in the promises of God.

About the Authors

L arry and Tiz Huch are the pastors of DFW New Beginnings in Irving, Texas. Founded in November 2004, this nondenominational church has quickly developed into a diverse, multiethnic congregation of several thousand people. The Huchs' dynamic ministry spans more than thirty years and two continents, and their international television program, *New Beginnings*, is broadcast weekly to millions of homes around the globe. The couple is wholeheartedly committed to bridging the gap between Christians and Jews and restoring the church to its Judeo-Christian roots.

Pastor Larry is a pioneer in the area of breaking family curses, which is the subject of his books *Free at Last* and *10 Curses That Block the Blessing*. He is also an ardent student of the Jewish roots of Christianity, which motivated him to write his latest books, *The Torah Blessing* and *Unveiling Ancient Biblical Secrets*.

Pastor Tiz, the successful author of several books, including *No Limits, No Boundaries*, is a frequent speaker at seminars and conferences throughout the world. Her practical yet personal teaching focuses on living the abundant life in marriage, family, personal relationships, business, and finances. Tiz also created the Women's Business Network to promote the entrepreneurial pursuits of Christian women.

Pastors Larry and Tiz are the proud parents of three wonderful children (and a terrific son-in-law and daughter-in-law), all of whom are active in ministry. Their three grandchildren, the "Sugars," are the loves of their lives.